In memoriam Marcel Sigrist

Christophe Rico, Jan Safford, Asterios E. Kechagias

One, Two, Three: Visual and Sequential Spoken Akkadian

One, Two, Three: Visual and Sequential Spoken Akkadian
by Christophe Rico, Jan Safford, Asterios E. Kechagias

Translated by the Polis Institute Press

Illustrations by Pau Morales and Denis Coutier
Design and Layout by Lloyd Schroeder

ISBN: 978-965-7698-21-1

press@polisjerusalem.org
www.polisjerusalem.org
8 HaAyin Het St, 9511208 Jerusalem, Israel

Polis Institute Press is a subsidiary of Polis – The Jerusalem Institute of Languages and Humanities.

I

Index

TABLE OF CONTENTS

2 DEICTICS, MOVEMENTS AND BODY PARTS

3 DESCRIBING THE WORLD

I Foreword

INTRODUCTION

But for the strange paths and by-ways of history, Akkadian might well have been one of the classical languages of a modern world that saw its roots in the Tigris and Euphrates River Valleys in what is today Iraq, rather than the much later peninsulas and islands of Italy and Greece. Today it is easy to forget that for over two and a half millennia, from sometime early in the third millennium BCE to sometime around the time of Alexander the Great, and perhaps even later in small remnant communities, Akkadian, an East-Semitic cousin language of Hebrew, Arabic, and Aramaic, was the dominant international and academic language of the entire Middle East, from Egypt to today's Iran, and from the Hittite realm in Anatolia down to the biblical Holy Land. Unfortunately, the end of the Bronze Age saw the replacement of Akkadian and its cuneiform script as the dominant form of writing in the Ancient Near East by the alphabet and the rise of Aramaic. With the fall of the Neo-Babylonian Empire of Nebuchadnezzar II in 539 BCE, Akkadian too lost its political power. Yet, Akkadian lived on in spoken form in at least southern Iraq (Babylonia) for centuries, and in written form until at least the end of the first century CE when the latest group of dated documents finally peters out. Certainly by the time of Mohammed there were no more speakers of Akkadian, but by then Akkadian's last window of opportunity to live on as a liturgical language, for example, for use by a Babylon branch of the Eastern Church, had long since closed. So what is the purpose of this book?

One can cite many justifications for teaching spoken Akkadian as an academic endeavor in line with the Polis method of teaching ancient languages as living ones. Yet, this technical pedagogical answer to the question that I posed at the end of my opening paragraph seems to me incomplete. In truth, Akkadian never really died, even though its sounds and written cuneiform signs were almost completely forgotten. Akkadian, and its partner non-Semitic Ancient Mesopotamian language Sumerian lived and still live on through loan-words in Biblical Hebrew and Aramaic dialects, and even on into English ("abyss," for instance), but more importantly, basic forms and concepts of Western Civilization that had been expressed through Akkadian and by Akkadian speakers have continued onwards in Judeo-Christian-Islamic culture. Even our paradise, The Garden of Eden, is etymologically derived from two words/signs in the Sumerian-Akkadian repertoire, and our biblical Wisdom books and Genesis accounts have a long history of antecedents in the literature and world-view of the Akkadian speaking world of the Ancient Near East.

Of course, Akkadian will never again be a spoken language, unlike the modern revival dialects of Greek and Hebrew. For the Babylonians, there were no survivors like the Jewish communities of the diaspora who kept the sounds of Hebrew alive in prayer and learning from ancient times down to the present day. However, Akkadian has indeed come back to life in a roundabout way through the 19th century research that deciphered cuneiform and renewed the sounds of Akkadian and Sumerian, albeit altered by the accents of speakers whose mother tongues are the living languages of our world, and not the ancient world. Akkadian can be heard in the classrooms and lecture halls of today's universities and can be read and recited from the original cuneiform script by way of hundreds of thousands of cuneiform tablets that are to be found in collections, large and small, throughout Europe, North America, and the Middle East, and even as far away from ancient Babylon as the South Island of New Zealand. Thus, we can welcome this attempt to offer a different form of Akkadian than the traditional written Akkadian of modern universities, museums, and other institutions.

Anyone who has learned to speak a foreign language knows that speaking a language offers a whole different set of experiences than simply reading. I believe, or perhaps "hope" might be a more careful word here, that learning Akkadian as a spoken language will provide users of this book with a new, deeper understanding, or perhaps even a better sense of intimacy, with this most ancient and important language. With this in mind, may the sounds of Akkadian ring out in the courtyard of Polis in Jerusalem, and elsewhere worldwide wherever this novel experiment in teaching Akkadian as a spoken language may come to be found.

Prof. Wayne Horowitz

II Prologue

Jerusalem, as a city with a magnificent historical tradition, certainly has many different delights to offer to its residents and visitors alike. One of these unique jewels is the Polis Institute of Languages and Humanities. It is a school for languages that has set itself the unique goal of reviving ancient languages by teaching them as living languages. It is a very special project which is laden with inherent difficulties. It is not certain how most (if not all) ancient languages were actually pronounced at the time they were spoken, and scholars today do not always agree on fine points of grammar, syntax and vocabulary. Furthermore, because Akkadian was written in various places (Egypt, Israel, Syria, Turkey, Iraq) and for approximately 2,000 years, it consisted of many dialects which underwent various grammatical, syntactic and lexical changes (not to mention the changes in the writing system). If one were to take English as an example, although Chaucer lived less than 700 years ago, his English would only be understood by native speakers today with great difficulty; English from the 10th century and earlier, meanwhile, would be a completely foreign language. Most of the Akkadian vocabulary we possess is usually derived from administrative and literary texts left to us by kings and elites. We do not know much about what was going on at the same time among the common people, how their everyday dialogues were conducted, or if the language used by ordinary people was even the same as that recorded by scribes.

Nevertheless, despite all these difficulties, the Polis Institute's project, shared by others around the globe, is quite commendable. A teacher does not need psychological and pedagogical studies to prove that students do not all learn the same. While some students may be able to learn a language on their own by reading a grammar book with its esoteric jargon, other students who are primarily kinesthetic or aural learners need to engage with a language actively and playfully, much the same way a child naturally learns his mother tongue. While we do not expect students to read the *Enuma Elish* or *Gilgamesh* after one semester of spoken Akkadian, we do believe this book will enable many students to ease into the language and continue in more formal settings. Indeed, at the Polis Institute, after two years of spoken Ancient Greek classes, students can be heard debating Plato's dialogues in Ancient Greek. Elsewhere at Cambridge, meanwhile, "The Poor Man of Nippur" has recently been turned into a short movie conducted entirely in Akkadian. Perhaps in a few years students will not only watch the movie, but discuss it in Akkadian afterwards.

This textbook is a translation of the Spoken Latin textbooks already published by the Polis Institute. It is necessary to make some additional comments on the methodology we have followed in producing this translation. The first problem we faced was related to which dialect of the Akkadian Language and which form of the Akkadian cuneiform script to use. The term "*Akkadian Language*" is very broad, as several variations of it are attested both dialectically (Babylonian, Assyrian, Mari etc.) and chronologically (Old Babylonian, Standard Babylonian, Neo-Assyrian etc.). We very quickly found that the variety of vocabulary necessary, as well as the scarce availability of particular vocabulary at certain stages of the Akkadian language, made it impossible to restrict ourselves to a specific time period. Very often the words or grammatical phenomena we were looking for appear in different stages of the language and are not available in every stage. In view of this, we decided that, in terms of vocabulary and grammar, the reconstruction of spoken Akkadian that we would present would draw on material from many different stages of the language. However, in terms of the type of cuneiform writing, we chose Neo-Assyrian, not only because it is the most established, but mainly because it is generally the easiest for neophytes. Even the proper names we chose to use from the ancient Mesopotamian world, which were very often written using Sumerian or Old Babylonian cuneiform, were converted to Neo-Assyrian script wherever possible. In certain cases, however, and always in reference to proper names, a few wedges from earlier periods were retained. This was partly because there was no direct equivalent in the Neo-Assyrian version and partly because, like in many languages, proper names tend to preserve elements of historical spelling (e.g., the name Leicester in English). We decided to maintain this feature in Akkadian as well, to the extent that it does not pose difficulties for students. This will also provide students with an opportunity to become familiar with some older symbols and observe their differences from the Neo-Assyrian script.

A second problem that quickly arose was whether we should adhere exactly to the Neo-Assyrian way of writing or whether we should simplify it in certain points, in order to make it more understandable and easier for the students. The Akkadian language, as is well known, contains many different signs for the same or similar sounds. For example, there are many different symbols for the sound "*u*" (𒌋 𒌑 𒅇 u, u2, u3 = u, ú, ù). As can be seen from ancient sources, in some words there is a special preference of ancient writers as to which "u" to use. For instance, the "u" for the conjunction "*and*" is usually written "u3." Nevertheless, in order to avoid overwhelming students with all these conventions, we have decided to simplify the written form of Neo-Assyrian as much as possible. As a general rule, we have established that the first form of each syllable (e.g., qu, du as opposed to qú, dú) should be used. However, we have largely retained the conventions regarding the use of u, meaning that words containing a sole syllable u are always written with ú (e.g., urudûm is written as ú-ru-du-ú-um). This ensures that students become familiar with the existence of such conventions. During the course, the instructor will be able to inform students about the preferences of ancient authors regarding sign conventions. Each individual word is presented in syllabic form rather than through logograms.

In creating the syllables of each word, the established rules of Akkadian spelling were followed. In ancient texts, the length of vowels is usually not stated in writing. Parāšum is usually spelled as "*pa-ra-šu-um*" and not as "*pa-ra-a-šu-um.*" Sometimes, however, one observes that the circumflex is indicated. For example, "petûm" can be written as "*pe-tu-um*" but also as "*pe-tu-u-um.*" As a general rule, we have chosen not to indicate vowel length in order to remain closer to ancient practice. In some cases, however, we mark only the circumflex, allowing students to become familiar with this convention as well.

Regarding mimation and nunation at the end of words, which tend to disappear as the language progresses, we decided to keep them in the book for pedagogical reasons, given that it is an introductory textbook. In order to make the wedges more distinct, we added a space between them, so as not to confuse the student if they were written sticking together. However, we did not leave a space between words in sentence, since there were no punctuation marks in ancient Akkadian. The phrase "šipram ina bīt dayyānim eppeš. Dayyānum anāku (I work at the court of law. I am a judge)," is written without any punctuation marks, as follows:

A final problem that had to be solved was that this book is intended to revive the Akkadian language in the present, and therefore has to include vocabulary used today, not only that of Antiquity. A way had to be found to construct words in Akkadian such as telephone, cinema, car, and umbrella. In such cases, neologisms were derived through comparative Semitic linguistics. In other words, we looked at how the above words were rendered in modern Semitic languages such as Hebrew or Arabic and we imitated their logic as best as we could in Akkadian.

Some additional conventions that we followed are the following: words beginning with "ay" such as the vetitive particle, were spelled in Standard Babylonian as "a-a" but in earlier periods they were spelled as "a-ia". We decided to follow the second form, which is quite extensive in most stages of Akkadian and which is also convenient for words like "*ayyikī'am.*" A strong conjugation is usually indicated by a double apostrophe, like the verb form "*tele"i.*" In our book, this is spelled by repeating the preceding vowel, a practice found in all periods of the Akkadian language, rather than by adding the syllables "ḫa, ḫi, ḫe, ḫu" as was exclusively the case in the Old Babylonian period. Moreover, since words are also found where the apostrophe is simply a glide, as in "*ayyikī'am,*" and there the spelling happens only by repeating the preceding vowel and never with the syllables "*ḫa, ḫi, ḫe, ḫu,*" we decided to create a uniformity by following the same practice in strong conjugations. Therefore "ayyikī'am" will be spelled as "*a-ia-ki-a-am.*"

Given the gaps in our knowledge of exactly how Akkadian was used in Antiquity, especially in oral communication, we are not in a position to know for certain how reliable the reconstruction we have attempted is, nor whether we have chosen the right conventions. Nevertheless, while we are certain that many mistakes will be found in our translations, we hope that this effort will produce fruitful discussion amongst scholars, in addition to attracting the attention of many students who might express an interest in learning this amazing ancient language.

Jan Safford and Asterios E. Kechagias

III Acknowledgments

When we embarked on this endeavor to first translate a spoken Hebrew book and then a spoken Latin book into Akkadian, we quickly found that we could easily translate complex sentences and grammar into Akkadian, but many simple things, such as "Thank you" were no where to be found in any standard grammar books or dictionaries. At first, when we translated the spoken Hebrew book into Akkadian, we made the terrible methodological flaw of attempting to reconstruct Akkadian based off of another Semitic language and proposed that "Thank you" in Akkadian might be "*ina pānīka ahaddu*" as a literal translation of the Hebrew "מודה אני לפניך". When we ran this (and various other ideas) by Hannes Leonhardt, he kindly responded with multiple pages of example sentences from actual private Akkadian correspondences to justify other ways of saying "*please*" "*thank you*" or "*sorry*" that are certainly much closer to how these concepts were actually expressed. For instance, regarding "thank you" Hannes provided many examples in which Person A wrote to Person B to state that he had received a gift from Person B. In these correspondences Person A who received the gift usually wrote to Person B "*mahar* ^{god}A *u* ^{god}B *lukrub(ak)ka* = I will pray for you before god A and god B." Hannes suggested that for all intents and purposes this was functioning as "*Thank you*" and that "such formulae could conceivably be shortened to *lukrub!*, *lukrubakka!*" We are very grateful for all of Hannes' comments and help with ensuring that the Akkadian is much closer idiomatically to what a "native" might say rather than a simple translation.

A huge thank you also goes to Yigal Bloch who edited the spoken Akkadian book for us and found more typos than we care to admit. Yigal also helped us with coining new words such as "*telephone*." Originally, we proposed rigrêqum = "*farvoice*" but Yigal pointed out that compound nouns (which are very common in German) are extremely rare in Akkadian, so he proposed *rāgim nesûtim* = "*distance shouter*."

Special thanks also go to Elnathan Weissert and Wayne Horowitz who in addition to being our Akkadian teachers were constantly pestered by us with questions through this entire project.

Finally, we would like to thank North-West University of Potchefstroom in South Africa for providing substantial support and assistance, which made it possible to complete this book.

Lukrubakkunūti!

Jan Safford and Asterios E. Kechagias

IV Cuneiform Sign List

Cuneiform sign	Transliteration	Remarks
𒀀	a	
𒀊	ab, ap	
𒀜	ad, at, aṭ	
𒄴	aḫ	
𒀝	ak	
𒀠	al	
𒂔	am	
𒀭	an	
𒅈	ar	
𒀸	aš	
𒊍	az	
𒁀	ba	
𒁁	be	
𒁉	bi	
𒁍	bu, pu	
𒁲	di, de	
𒁺	du	
𒂊	e	
𒅎	em, im	
𒂗	en	
𒅁	ep	
𒂵	ga	
𒈪	gi6, mi, me	gi6 is the logogram for "night"
𒄩	ḫa	

Value	Note
ḫe, ḫi	
ḫu	
i	
eb, ib	
ik	
il	
im, em	
ir, er	
iṣ	
iš	
iṭ	
iz	
ka	
ku	
la	
le, li	
lu	
ma	
mi, me, gi6	gi6 is the logogram for "night"
mu	
na	
ni	
nu	
pa	
pu, bu	
qu	
ra	
ri, re	
ru	

se, si	
ša	
še	
ši, lim	
šu	
ta	
te	
ti	
tu	
ṭa	
ṭi	
ṭu	
u	
u4, ud, ut, uṭ	u4 is the logogram for “day”
ub	
ul	
um	
up	
uš	
wa, we, wi, wu	
ya, ye, yi, yu	
za	
zi	

mu	ma	mi	me	m	um	am		im/em	
bu	ba	bi	be	b	ub, up	ab, ap		ib/eb, ip/ep	
pu	pa	pi/pe		p					
tu	ta	ti	te	t	ut, uṭ, ud	at, aṭ, ad		it/et, iṭ/eṭ, id/ed	
ṭu	ṭa	ṭi/ṭe		t					
du	dú	Dù	da	d					
šu	šú	Ša	šá	š	uš	aš	áš	iš	eš
su	sa	si/se		s	us/uṣ/uz	as/aṣ/az		is/iṣ/iz	
ṣu	ṣa	ṣi/ṣe		ṣ					

zu	za	zi/ze		z				
nu	na	ni	ne	n	un	an	in	en
lu	la	Li		l	ul	al	il	el
ru	ra	ri/re		r	ur	ar	ir	
gu	ga	gi/ge		g	ug/uk/uq	ag/ak/aq	ig/ik/iq	
ku	ka	ki/ke		k				
qu	qa	qi/qe		q				
hu	ha	hi		h	uh = ah = eh	‘ (glottal-stop)		
u	ú	ù			a	i		

	Ca	Ce	Ci	Cu	aC	eC	iC	uC
k								
g								
q								
p								
b								
t								
d								
m								
n								
s								
z								
ṣ								
š								
h								
l								
r								
y								
'								
w								

1 Paniš

FIRST THINGS FIRST

A TAḪDÂTUM — GREETINGS

Sîn-aḫḫē-erība

Bunnannītu

1 FIRST THINGS FIRST

A GREETINGS

Ūmum

Šērkum lū ṭāb
Lū šalmāta
Lū šalmāta

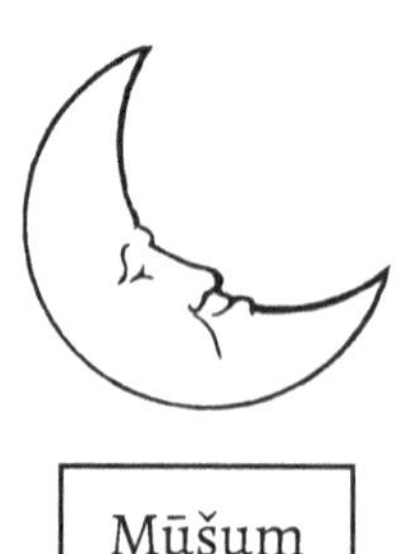

Mūšum

Lū šalmātunu
Lū šalmāta
Lū šalmāta

Lū šalmāta
Lū šalmāta
Lū šalmātunu

Lū šalmāta
Lū šalmāta
Lū šalmātunu

Maš'altum

Šulumka qibiam!

Gabrû

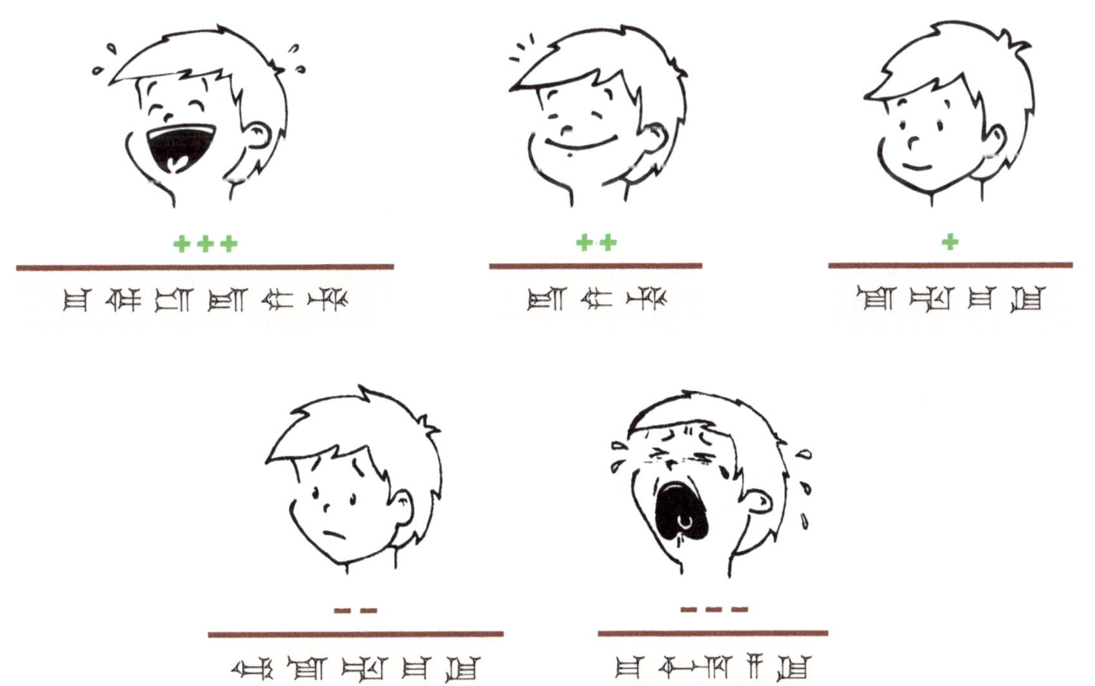

B ANĀKU, ATTA/ATTI, ANNIKĪ'AM, ULLĪKĪ'AM

I, YOU, HERE, THERE

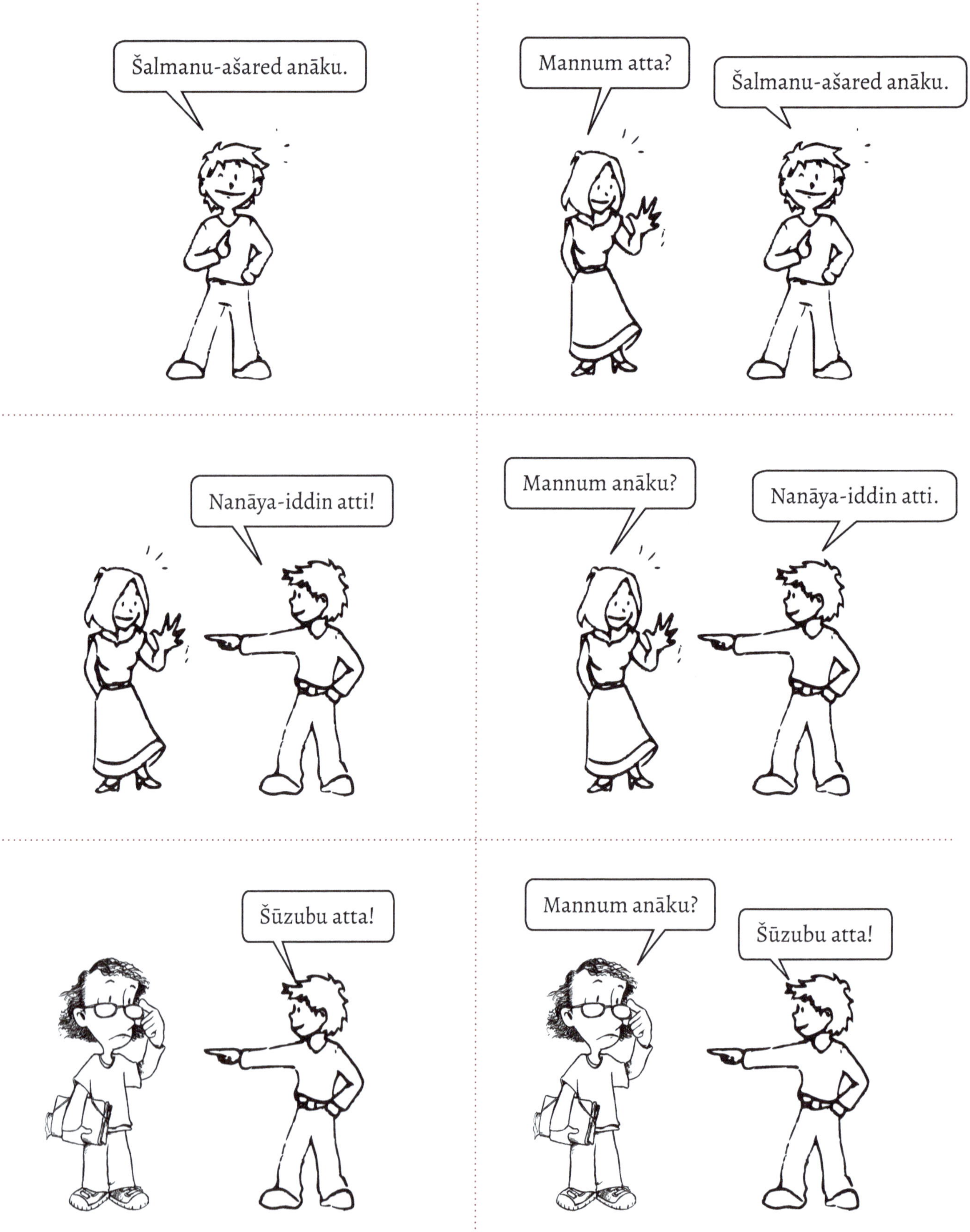

Šalmanu-ašared anāku.

Mannum atta?

Šalmanu-ašared anāku.

Nanāya-iddin atti!

Mannum anāku?

Nanāya-iddin atti.

B I, YOU, HERE, THERE

Tibe!
Atallak!
Izīz!
Šib!

Tibe!
Lusum!
Izīz!
Šib!

Tibe!
Atallak!
Ṣi!
Nērebum

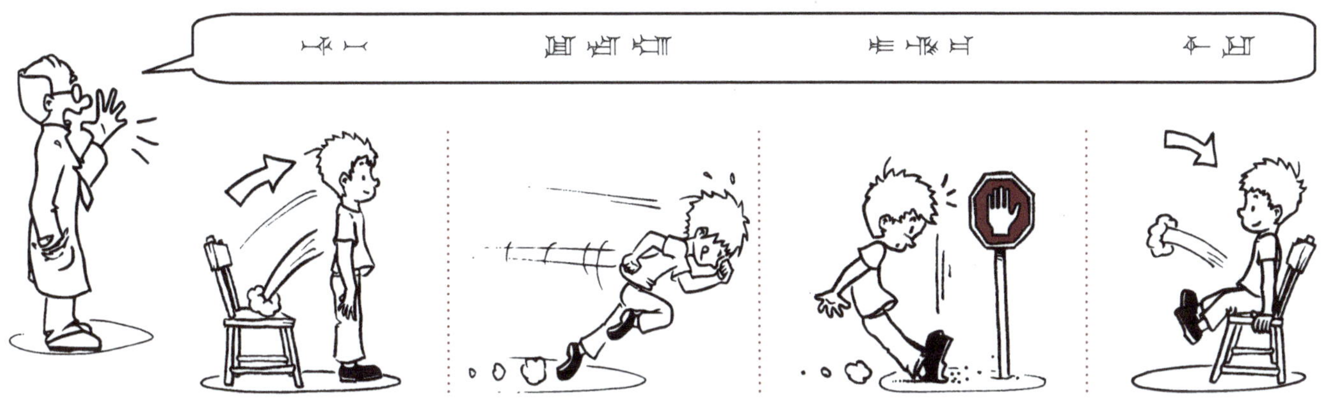

Annikī'am šib
Ullīkī'am šib
Alkam
Ullîšam alik
Annîšam lusmam
Ullîšam lusum

annûm → / ← ullûm

Ayyikī'am atta Šūzubu?
Annikī'am anāku
Ayyikī'am atti Bunnannītu?
Annikī'am anāku
Ayyikī'am anāku Šūzubu?
Ullikī'am atti Bunnannītu!
Ayyikī'am anāku, Bunnannītu?
Ullikī'am atta, Šūzubu

D QUESTIONS & ANSWERS

Anna

ŠALMANU-AŠARED

ŠŪZUBU

Ulla

ŠŪZUBU

SÎN-AḪḪĒ-ERĪBA

Lū Šūzubu lū
Sîn-aḫḫē-erība atta?

Alkam

Ullîšam alik

Tūram!

Ana paššūrim ṭiḫeam

Ana lē'im alkam

Ana aptim alkam

Ana daltim alkam

F IMPERATIVES OF MOTION

Ana paššūrim alik!

Ana lē'im alik!

Ana aptim alik

Ana daltim alik

Ana kussîka tūr

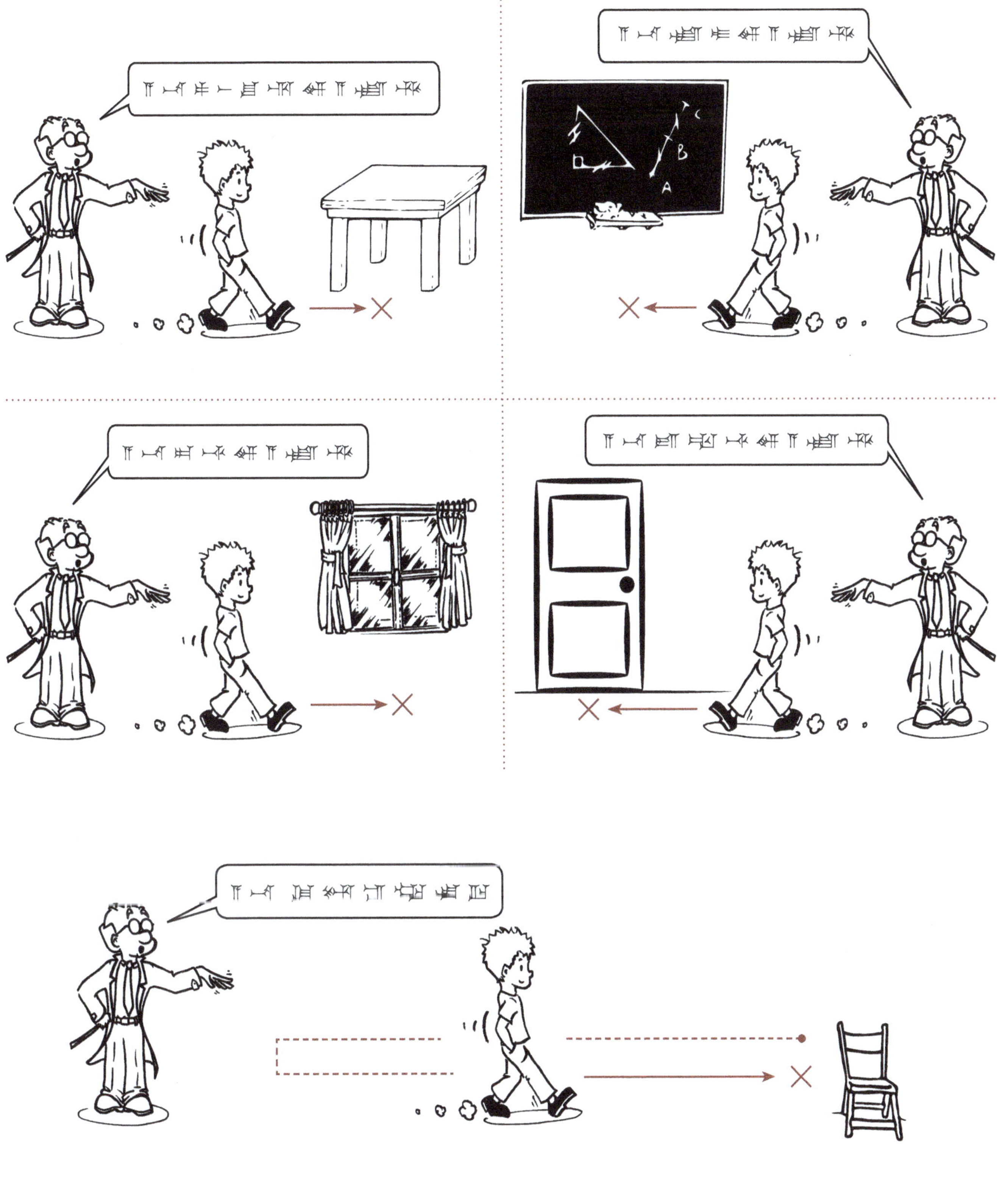

Nēẖiš
Arẖiš
Nēẖiš atallak
Arẖiš atallak
Nēẖiš šib
Arẖiš šib
Nēẖiš lusum
Arẖiš lusum

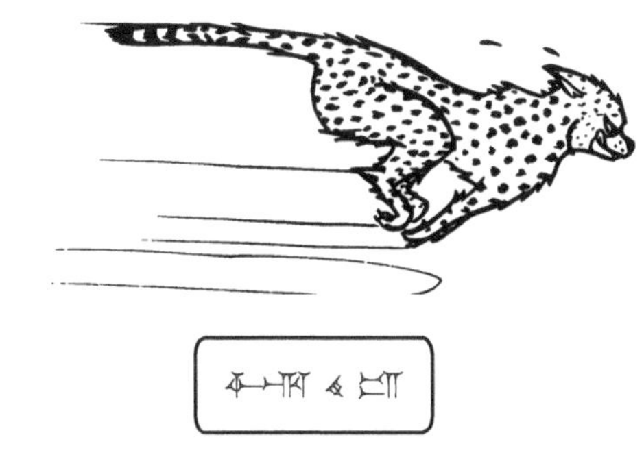

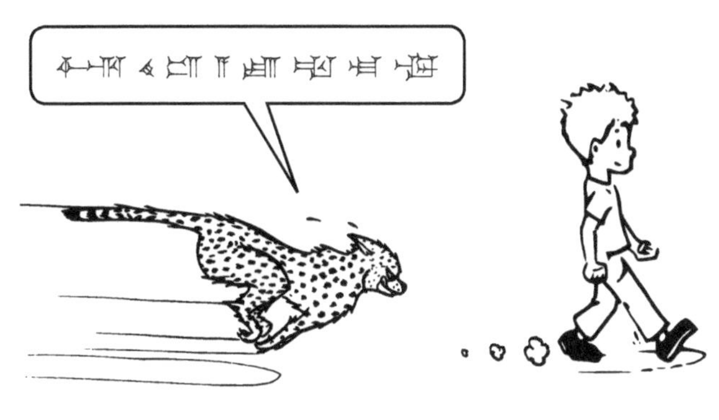

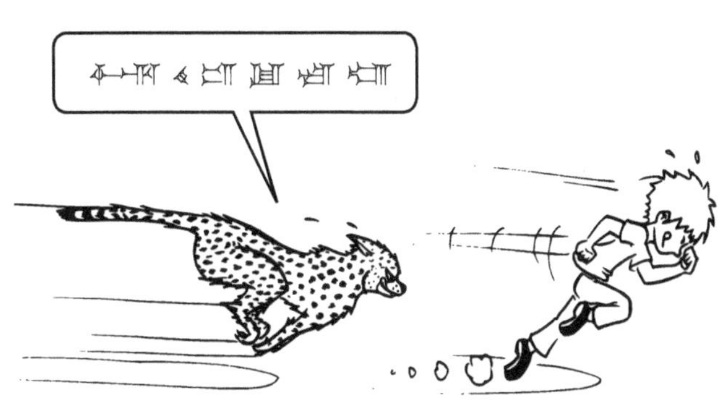

1

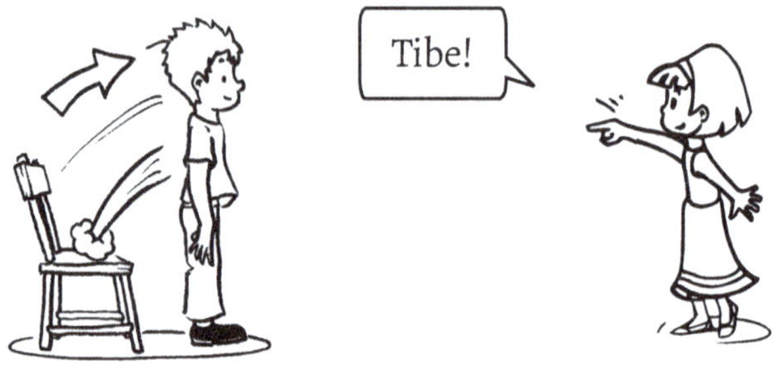

Tibe!

2

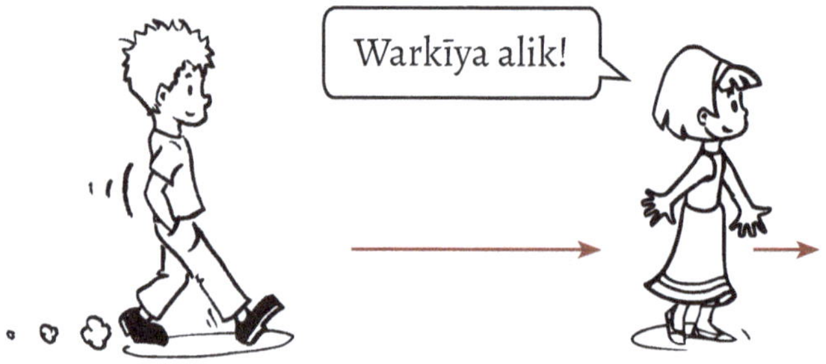

Warkīya alik!

3

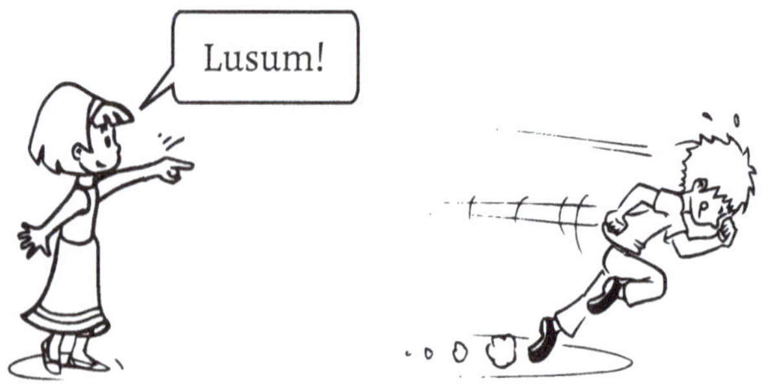

Lusum!

4

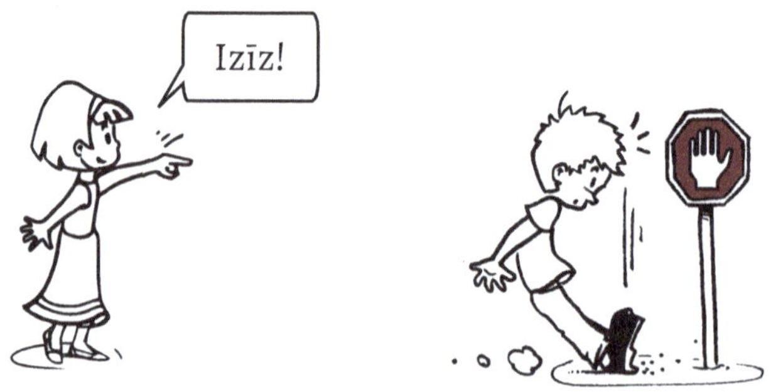

Izīz!

1

2

3

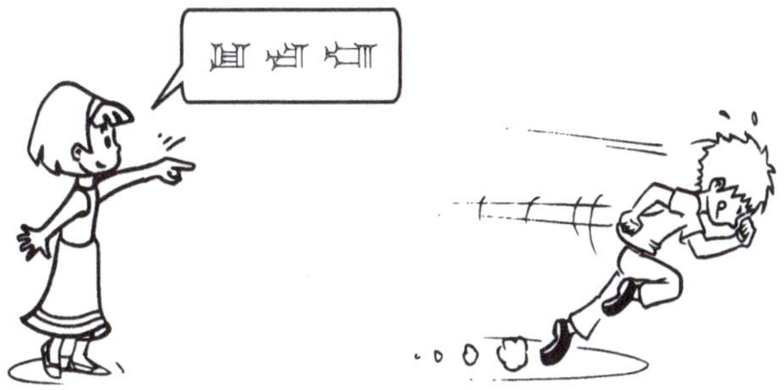

4

Ana šumēlim

Ana imnim

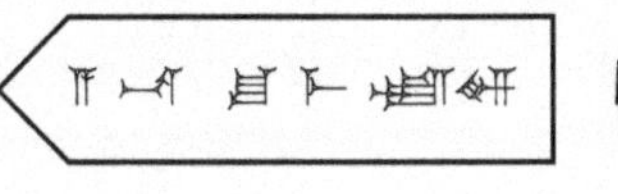

1

Lū imnum
lū šumēlum?
Ana imnim suḫur!

2

1

Tibe!

2

Warkīya alik!

1

Nabalkit!

2

Atallak !

1

2

1

2

1

2

ANNIKĪ'AM

IŠTU ULLÎŠAM

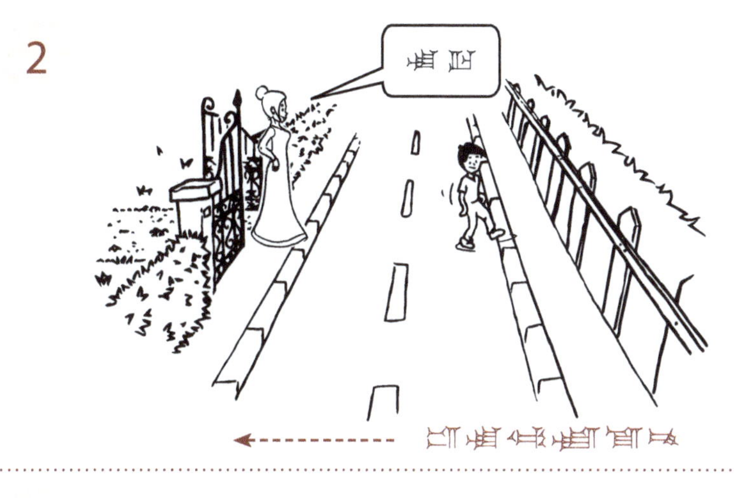

Mīnum annûm?
Ṭuppum.
Annûm ṭuppum?
Anna, ṭuppum annûm.
Mīnum annûm?
Qanṭuppum annûm.
Annûm qanṭuppum?
Anna, qanṭuppum annûm.
Mīnum annûm?
Naruqqum annītum.
Annītum naruqqum?
Anna, naruqqum annītum.

G

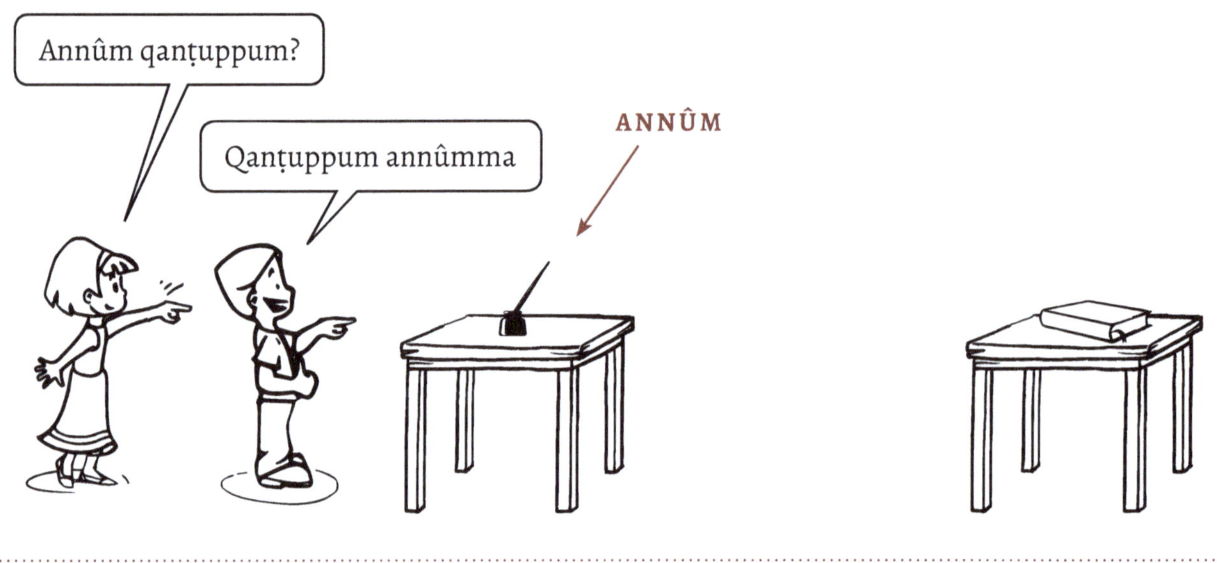

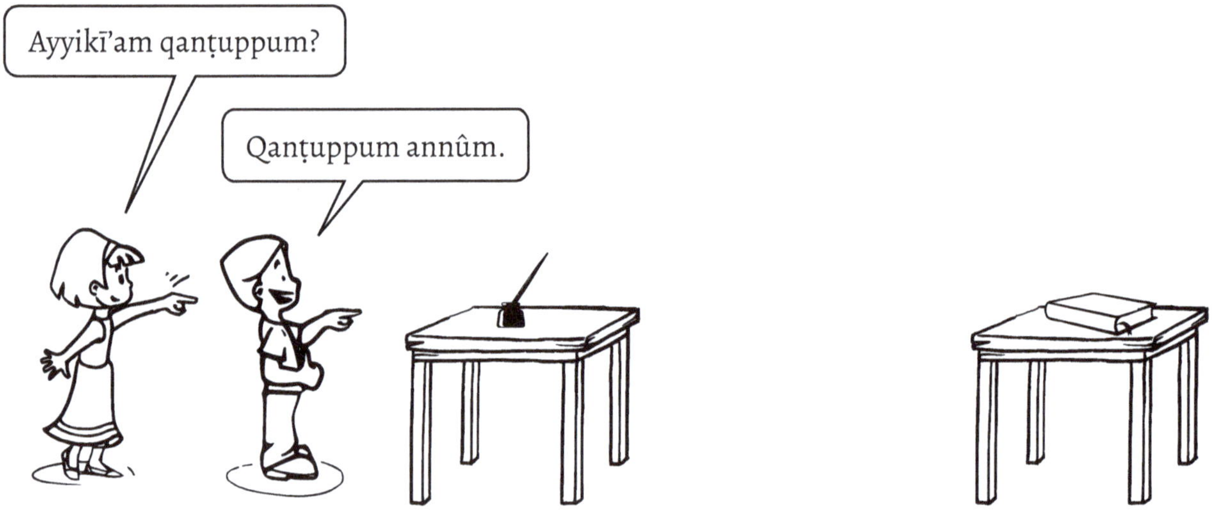

Ayyikī'am qanṭuppum?

Qanṭuppum annûm.

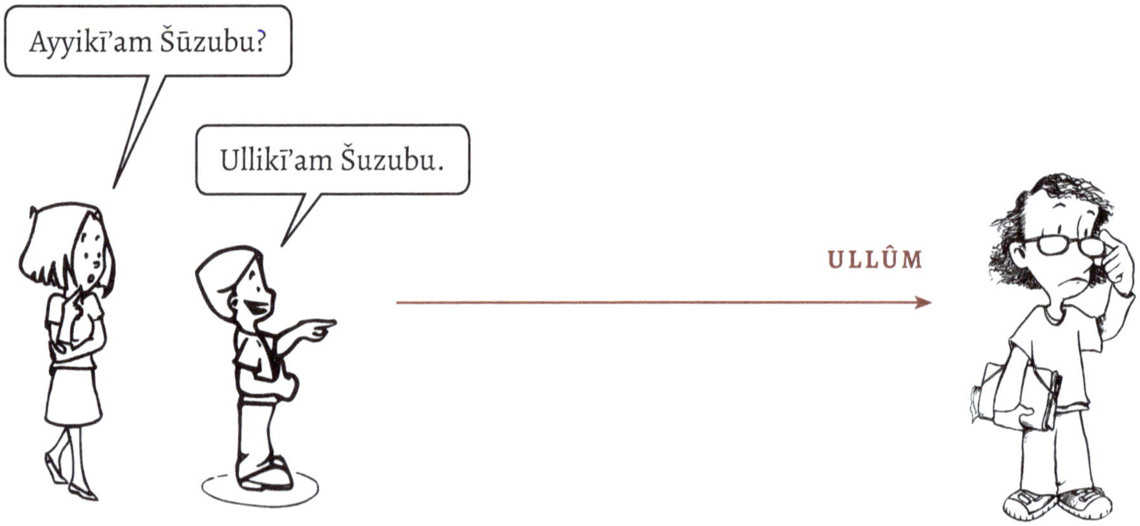

Ayyikī'am Šūzubu?

Ullikī'am Šuzubu.

ULLÛM

Šalmanu-ašared **anāku**

Šalmanu-ašared **atta** Nanāya-iddin **atti**

Aššur-bāni-apli **šū** Bunnanītum **šī**

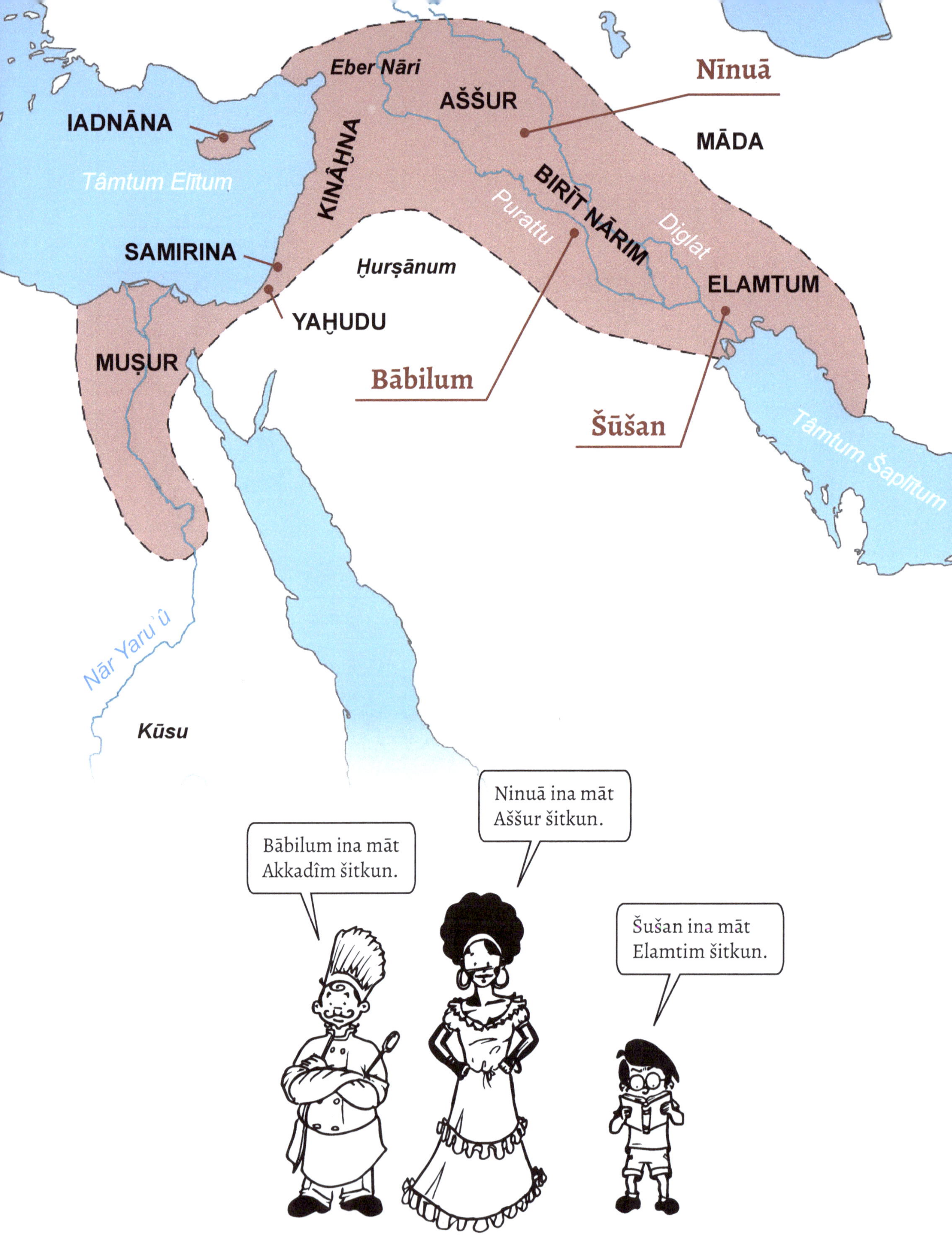
Eber Nāri
AŠŠUR
Nīnuā
MĀDA
IADNĀNA
KINÂḪNA
Tâmtum Elītum
BIRĪT NĀRIM
Purattu
Diglat
SAMIRINA
Ḫurṣānum
ELAMTUM
YAḪUDU
MUṢUR
Bābilum
Šūšan
Tâmtum Šapiltum
Nār Yaru'û
Kūsu
Bābilum ina māt Akkadîm šitkun.
Ninuā ina māt Aššur šitkun.
Šušan ina māt Elamtim šitkun.

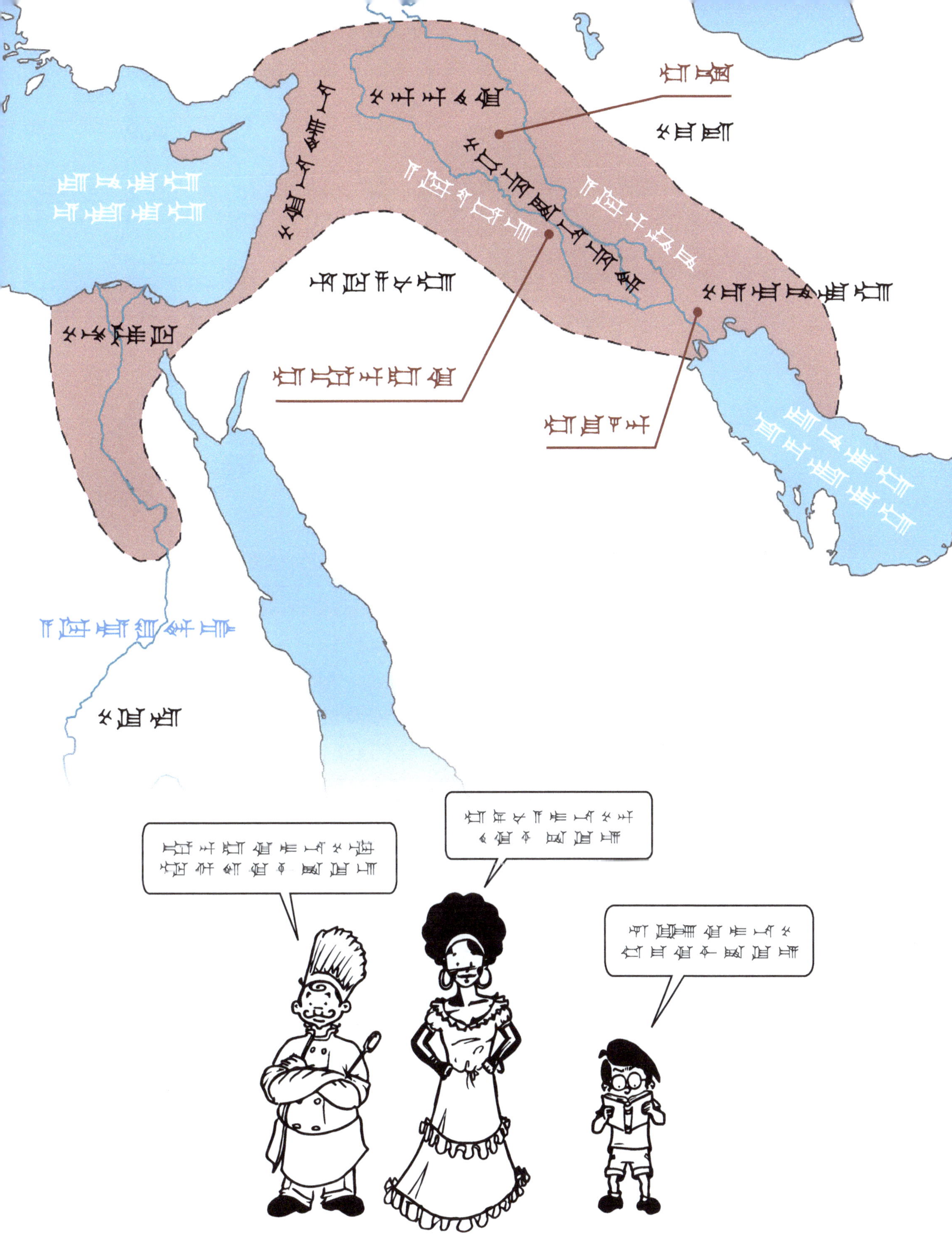

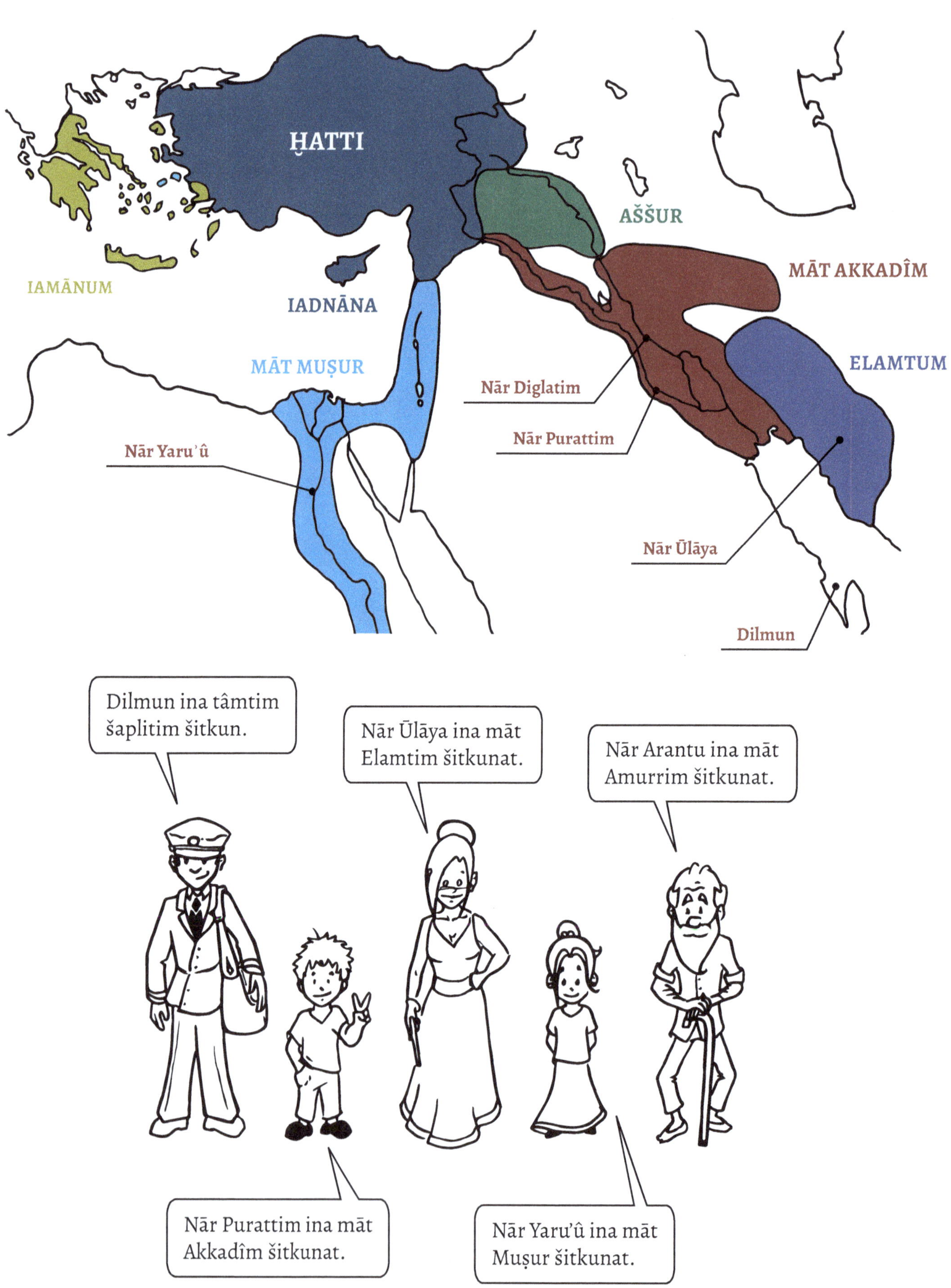
ḪATTI
AŠŠUR
MĀT AKKADÎM
IAMĀNUM
IADNĀNA
MĀT MUṢUR
ELAMTUM
Nār Diglatim
Nār Purattim
Nār Yaru'û
Nār Ūlāya
Dilmun
Dilmun ina tâmtim šaplitim šitkun.
Nār Ūlāya ina māt Elamtim šitkunat.
Nār Arantu ina māt Amurrim šitkunat.
Nār Purattim ina māt Akkadîm šitkunat.
Nār Yaru'û ina māt Muṣur šitkunat.

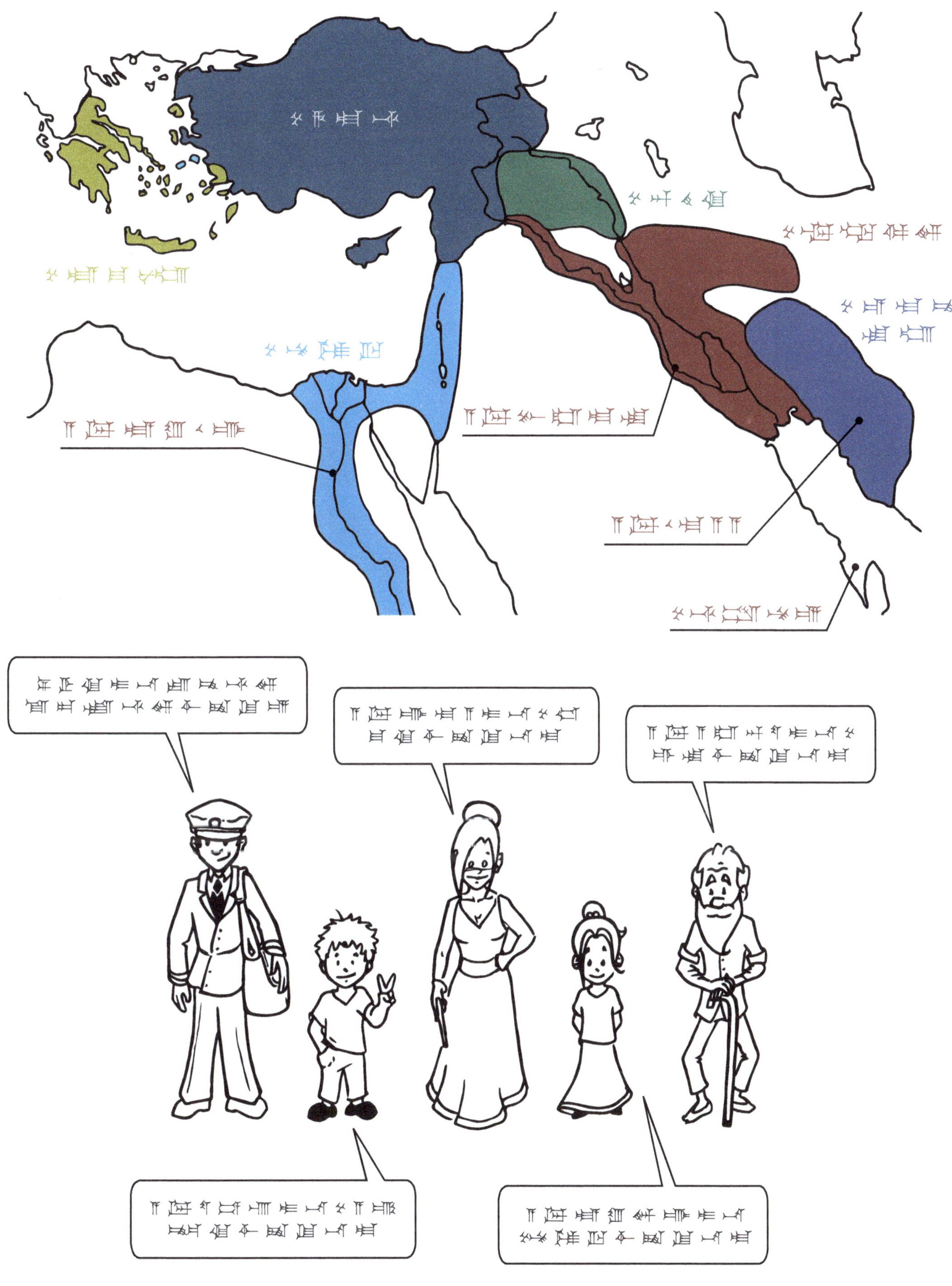

"APPUM"
MĪNUM?

Ina lišānim
akkadītim kī qabi?
?
Šamšum

Šalmānum-ašared u Nanaya-iddin nīnu

Mannum attunu?
Šalmanu-ašared u Nanāya-iddin nīnu

Šalmanu-ašared u Nanāya-iddin attunu?

Mannum nīnu?
Šalmanu-ašared u
Nanāya-iddin attunu.

Nanāya-iddin u Ballilītum attina.

Mannum nīnu?
Nanāya-iddin u
Ballilītu attina.

Šalmanu-ašared u Nanāya-iddin nīnu (we, male and female)

Šalmanu-ašared u Nanāya-iddin attunu (you pl. male and female)

Nanāya-iddin u Ballilītu attina (you pl. Female Female)

Aššur-bāni-apli u Sîn-aḫ̮ḫ̮ē-erība šunu (they, male male)

Nanāya-iddin u Ballilītu šina (they, female female)

Ayyikī'am māt Akkadī?
Akkad āl Akkadī ina māt Irāqi.
māt Akkadī
Aššur
Ayyikī'am Aššur?
Māt Akkadī ina māt Irāqi.

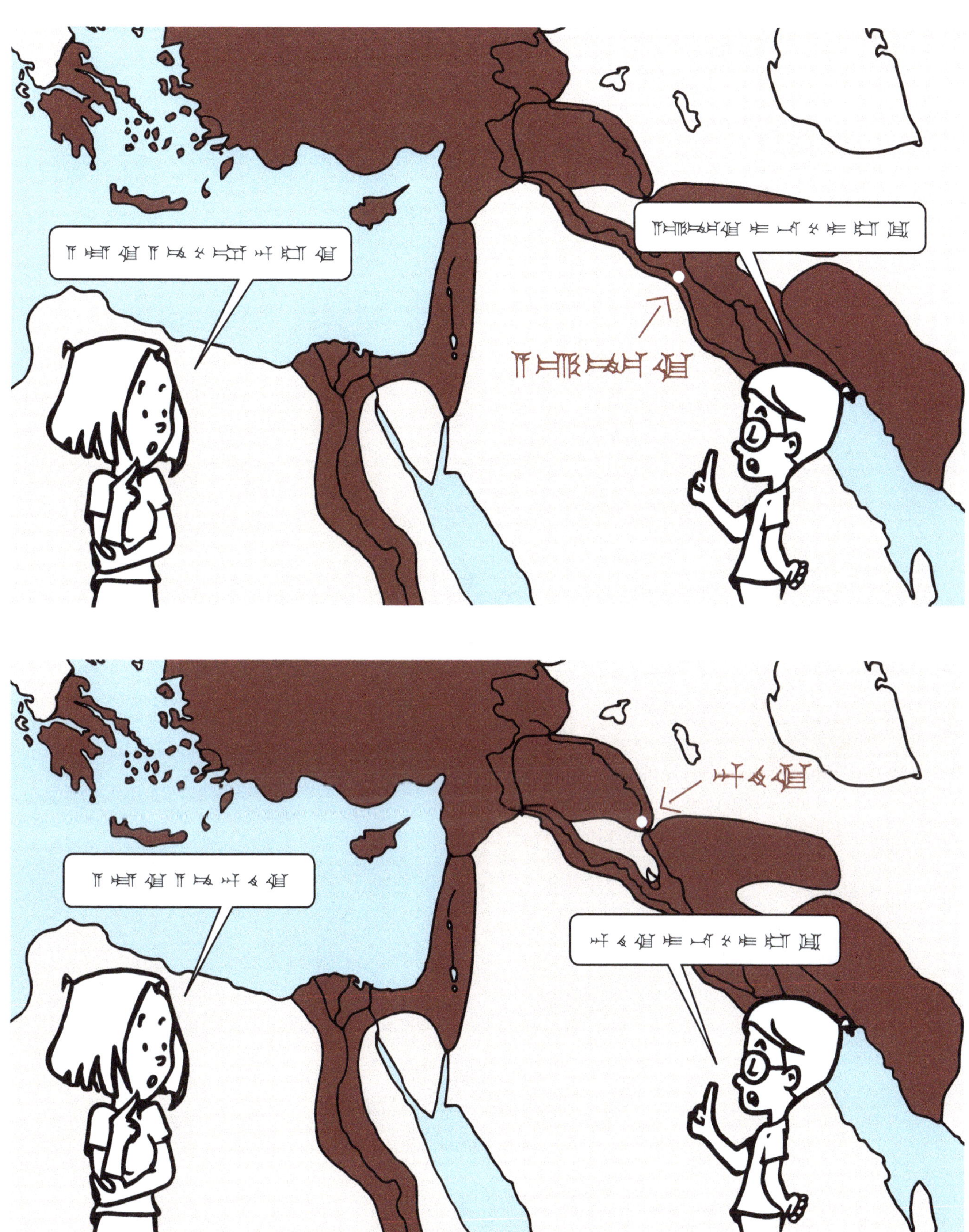

Ayyikī'am qanṭuppum?
Qanṭuppum ina naruqqim.
Ayyikī'am ṭuppum.
Ṭuppum ina naruqqim.
Ayyikī'am kāsum.
Kāsum ina quppim.

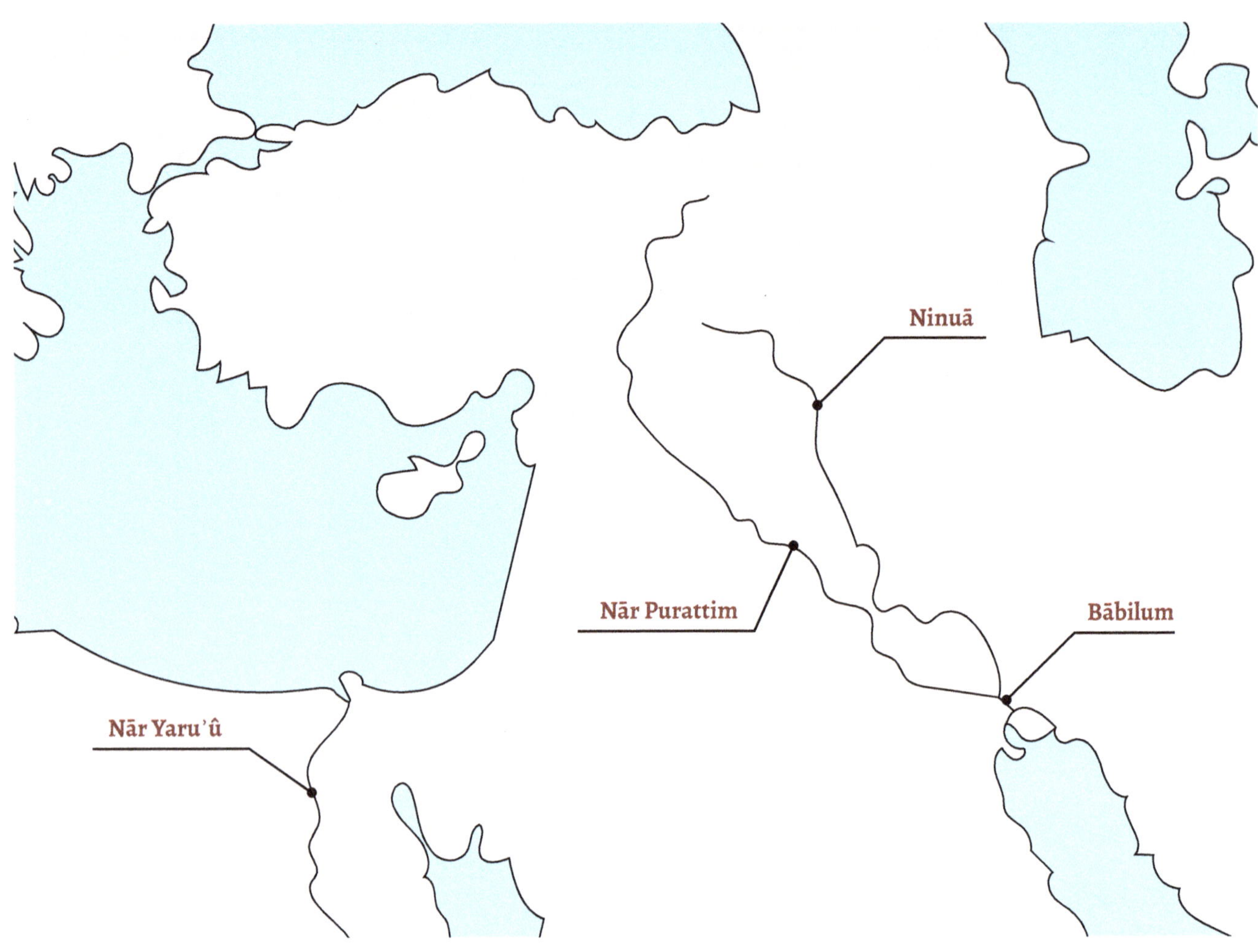

Bābilum ina māt Akkadîm šitkun

Ninuā ina māt Aššur šitkun

Šušim ina māt Elamtim šitkun

Dilmun ina tāmtim šaplitim šitkun

Nār **Purattim** ina māt Akkadîm šitkunat

Nār **Ūlāya** ina māt Elamtim šitkunat

Nār **Yaru'û** ina māt Miṣir šitkunat

Nār **Arantu** ina māt Amurrim šitkunat

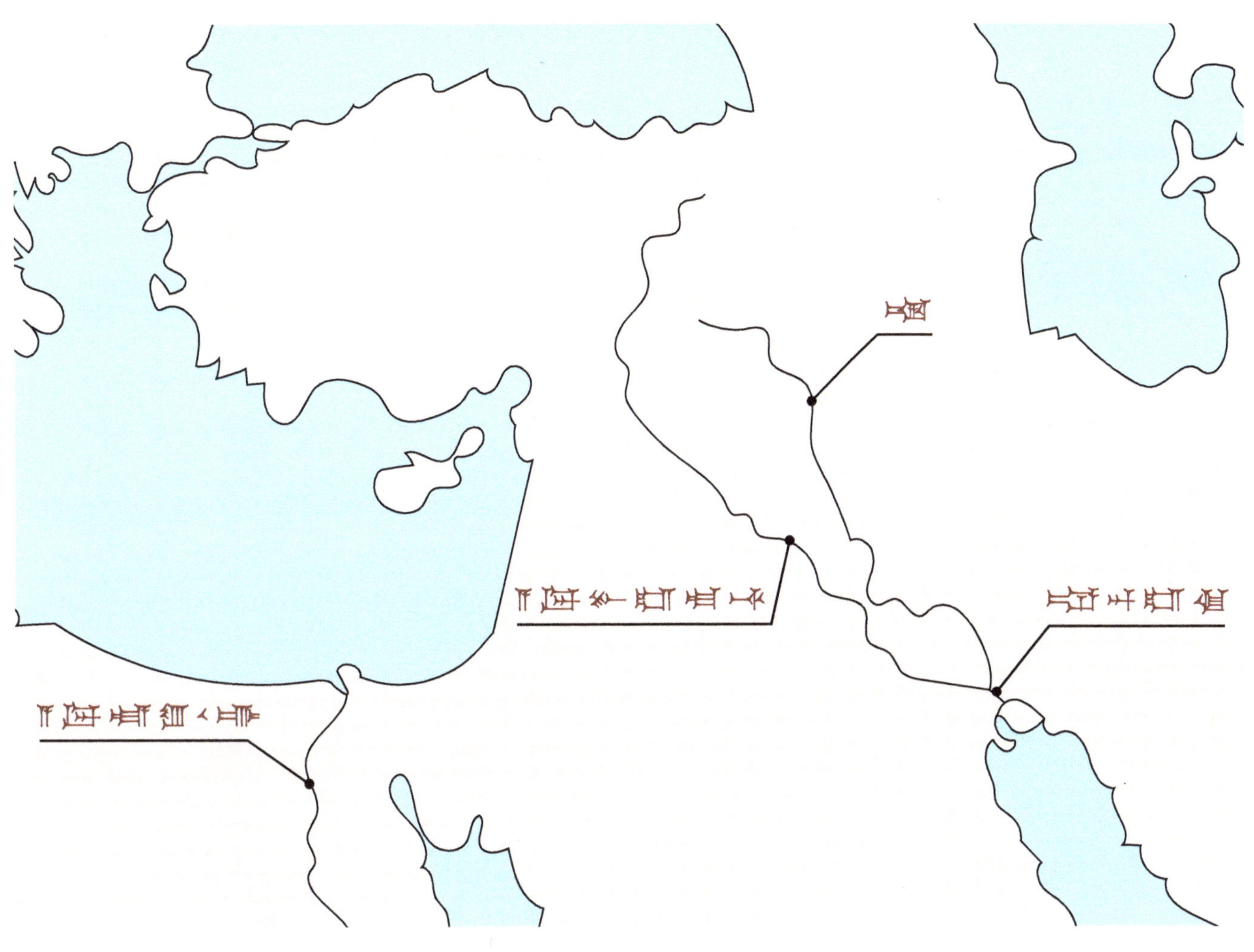

Mīnum annûm?
Annītum kussûm?
Ulla kussûmma paššūrum
Mīnum annûm?
Annûm qanṭuppum?
Ulla qanṭuppumma ṭuppum.
Rāgim nesûtim annûm?
Ulla rāgim nesûtimma qanṭuppum.

Annûm mārum?
Ulla mārumma mārtum.
Annītum mārtum?
Ulla mārtumma mārum.
Ullûm qanṭuppum?
Annûmma
qanṭuppum ula ullûm.
ANNÛM
ULLÛM
Ṭuppum annûm?
Ullûmma ṭuppum
ula annûm.
ANNÛM
ULLÛM

$E=MC^2$
$E=MC^2$

Mīnam eleqqe?
Qanṭuppam aḫuz.

Aḫussu.

Mīnam eleqqe?
Ṭuppam aḫuz.

Aḫussu.

Mīnam eleqqe?
Rāgim nesûtim aḫuz.

Aḫussu.

Ḫašḫūram liqe!
Ḫašḫūram akul!
Kāsam liqe!
Šiti!

Kāsam liqe!
Īṣam šiti!

Kāsam liqe!
Mādam šiti!

1

2

3

V AWĀTUM

urudûm

1

2

3

V

Šizbam šiqīni.
Šumma libbaka.
Lukrubakka.
Šumma libbaka.
Libbaka lā inakkud.
Aḫṭi

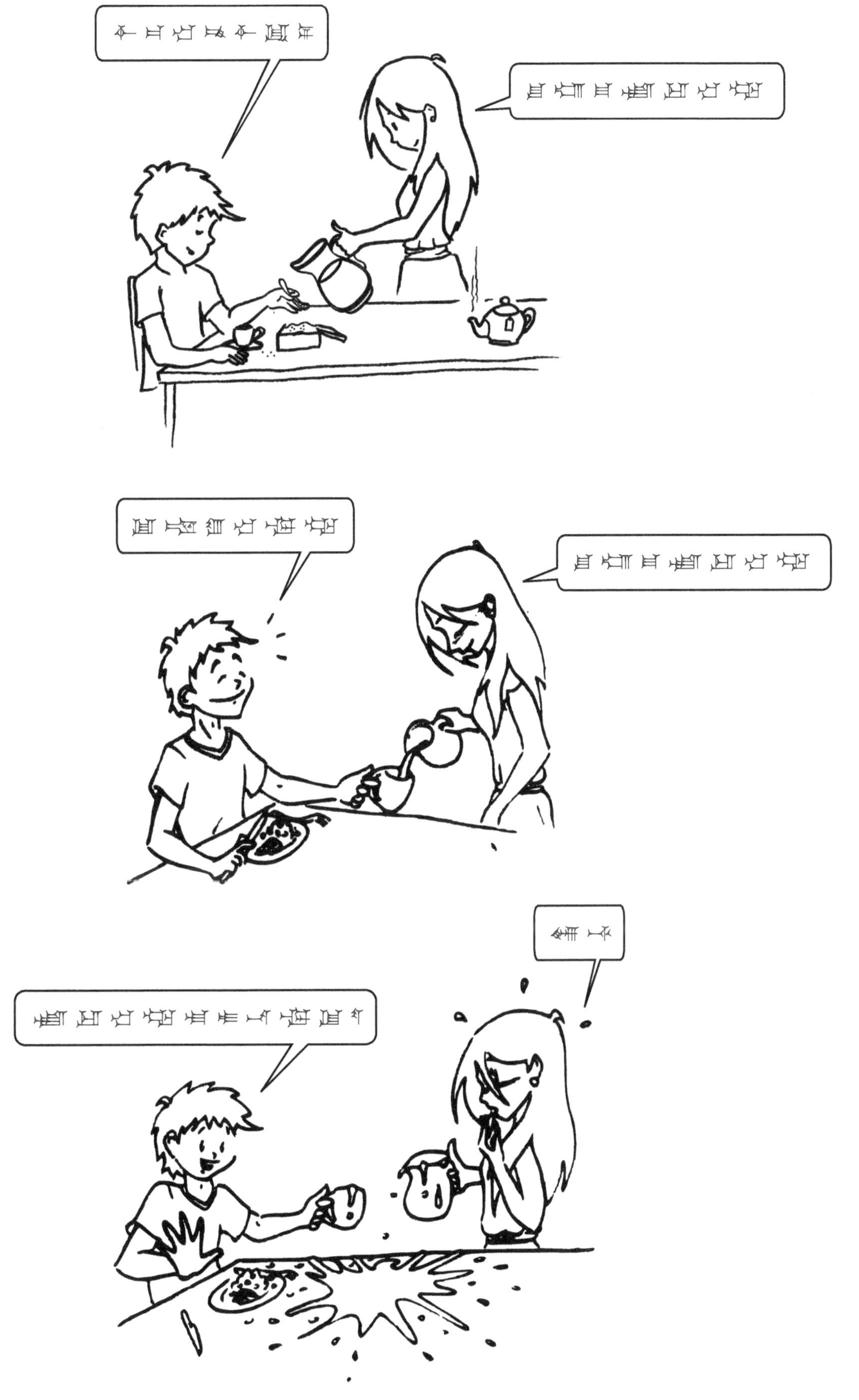

1
Talmīdū, Šamallû, šimeā!
2
Amat-Ninlil tešemmî?
3
Ummiānum, ešemme!
Akkadītam i nidbub!
1
Bābilum damqat
Šamaš-mudammiq, akkadītam tadabbub?
Annû, ummiānum. Akkadītam adabbub.
2
Ingalītam dabābum.
Paransitam dabābum.
Yaunītam dabābum.
Cheerio, my chap!
Vive la France!
Πῶς ἔχεις;
1
Šamšam eṣir
2
Mīnam teṣṣir?
Šamšam eṣṣir.

1
2
3
1
2
Cheerio, my chap!
Vive la France!
Πῶς ἔχεις;
1
2

1

Šamaš-mudammiq,
"Šamaš-mudammiq" qibi!
Šamaš-mudammiq.

2

Qibiā "@?#$"!
@? #$!

1

Babilam qibia!
Babilam

2

Šamaš-mudammiq,
"Gilgameš" qibi!
Gilgameš

1

Mīnum annûm?
Šamšum

2

Mīnum taqabbi?
?
Šamšum.
Anniam aqabbi.

1

2

1

2

1

2

1

2

3

Ahhē-iddin-Marduk, tallam šapal santakkī TU TA TI pirik!

Bītum

4

Mīnum teppeš?

Bītum

Tallam šapal santakkī TU TA TI aparrik.

5

1
2

3
4

5

1
Bēl-abu-uṣur ana lē'im alkam.
Bītum

2
Bēl-abu-uṣur, ša ina muḫḫi lē'im uṭul!
Mīnam tanaṭṭal?
Bītum
Awātam "Bītum" anaṭṭal.

3
Bēl-abu-uṣur, lē'am šisi!
Mīnam tašassi?
Bītum
Awātam 'Bītum' ašassi.

4
Bēl-abu-uṣur awātam annītam taḫkim?
Bītum
Anniam ul īde.

5
Bēl-abu-uṣur pusus!
Mīnam tapassas?
Bīt
Awātam "bītum" apassas.

1

2

3

4

5

Independent personal pronouns:

1cs	anāku
2ms	atta
2fs	attī
3ms	šū
3fs	šī
1cp	nīnu
2mp	attunu
2fp	attina
3mp	šunu
3fp	šina

	Near Demonstratives (this, these)		**Far Demonstratives (that, those)**	
	masc.	**fem.**	**masc.**	**fem.**
singular nom.	annûm	annītum	ullûm	ullītum
gen.	annîm	annītim	ullîm	ullītim
acc.	anniam	annītam	ulliām	ullītam
plural nom.	annûtum	anniātum	ullûtum	ulliātum
g.-a.	annûtim	anniātim	ullûtim	ulliātim

	nom	**gen -acc**	**dat**
ms fs mp	šū	šuātu	šuāšim
fp	šī	šuāti	šuāšim
acc.	šunu	šunūti	šunūšim
plural nom.	šina	šināti	šināšim

	alākum	alākum + am	erēbum	waṣûm	ezēbum	wašābum	tebûm
				Marû			
1cs	allak	allakam	errub	uṣṣi	ezzib	uššab	etebbe
2ms	tallak	tallakam	terrub	tuṣṣi	tezzib	tuššab	tetebbe
2fs	tallakī	tallakīm	terrubī	tuṣṣî	tezzibī	tuššabī	tetebbî
3cs	illak	illakam	irrub	uṣṣi	izzib	uššab	itebbe
3cs	nillak	nillakam	nirrub	nuṣṣi	nizzib	nuššab	nitebbe
2cp	tallakā	tallakānim	terrubā	tuṣṣiā	tezzibā	tuššabā	tetebbeā
3mp	illakū	illakūnim	irrubū	uṣṣû	izzibū	uššabū	itebbû
3fp	illakā	illakānim	irrubā	uṣṣiā	izzibā	uššabā	itebbeā
				ṣit pî			
2ms	alik	alkam	erub	ṣi	ezib	šib	tebe
2fp	alkī	alkīm	erbī	ṣî	ezbī	šibī	tebî
2cp	alkā	alkānim	erbā	šiā	ezbā	šibā	tebeā

	qabûm	šemûm	amārum	petûm	peḫûm	nadānum	leqûm
				Marû			
1cs	aqabbi	ešemme	ammar	epette	epeḫḫe	anaddin	eleqqe
2ms	taqabbi	tešemme	tammar	tepette	tepeḫḫe	tanaddin	teleqqe
2fs	taqabbî	tešemmî	tammarī	tepettî	tepeḫḫî	tanaddinī	teleqqî
3cs	iqabbi	išemme	immar	ipette	ipeḫḫe	inaddin	ileqqe
3cs	niqabbi	nišemme	nimmar	nipette	nipeḫḫe	ninaddin	nileqqe
2cp	taqabbiā	tešemmeā	tammarā	tepetteā	tepeḫḫeā	tanaddinā	teleqqeā
3mp	iqabbû	išemmû	immarū	ipettû	ipeḫḫû	inaddinū	ileqqû
3fp	iqabbiā	išemmeā	immarā	ipetteā	ipeḫḫeā	inaddinā	ileqqeā
				ṣit pî			
2ms	qibi	šeme	amur	pete	peḫe	idin	leqe
2fp	qibî	šemî	amrī	petî	peḫî	idnī	leqî
2cp	qibiā	šemeā	amrā	peteā	peḫeā	idnā	leqeā

2 Taklīmū u tallaktu u zittū pagrim

DEICTICS, MOVEMENTS AND BODY PARTS.

A TAKLĪMU

DEICTICS SINGULAR

2

DEICTICS, MOVEMENTS AND BODY PARTS.

A

DEICTICS SINGULAR

Mīnum annītum?
E=MC²
Annītum talmittum.

Mīnum annītum?
Annītum sinništum.

Mīnum annûm?
Annītum naruqqum.

Mīnum annûm?
Annītum šamšum.

Mīnum annûm?
Annûm qanṭuppum.

Mīnum annûm?
NŪNUM
Annûm nūnum.

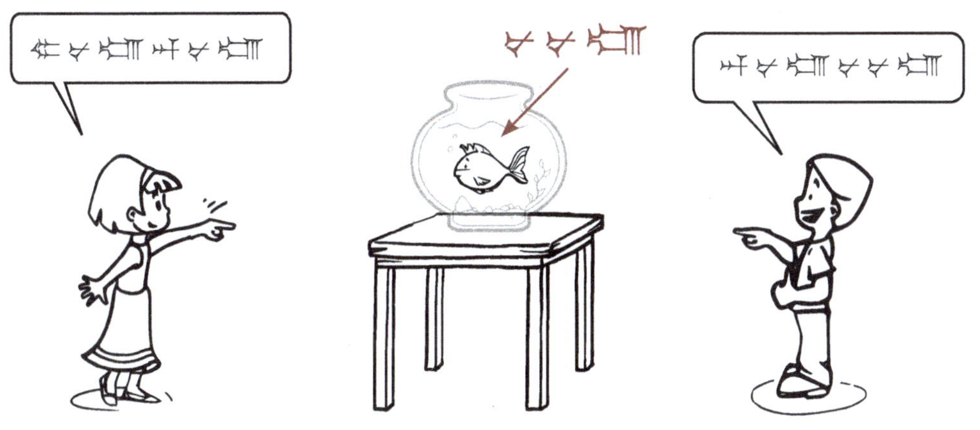

Mīnum annûm?
E=MC²
Annûm mulammidum.

Mīnum annûm?
E=MC²
Annûm(ma) talmīdum.

Mīnum annûm?
Annûm zikarum.

Mīnum annûm?
Annûm(ma) ṭuppum ṣeḫrum.
Mīnum annûm?
Annûm(ma) ṭuppum rabûm.
Mīnum annûm?
Annûm iṣurtum.

Mīnum annûm?
Annûm ḫašḫūrum.

Mīnum annûm?
Annītum kāsum.
Mīnum annûm?
Annītum ḫašḫaltum.

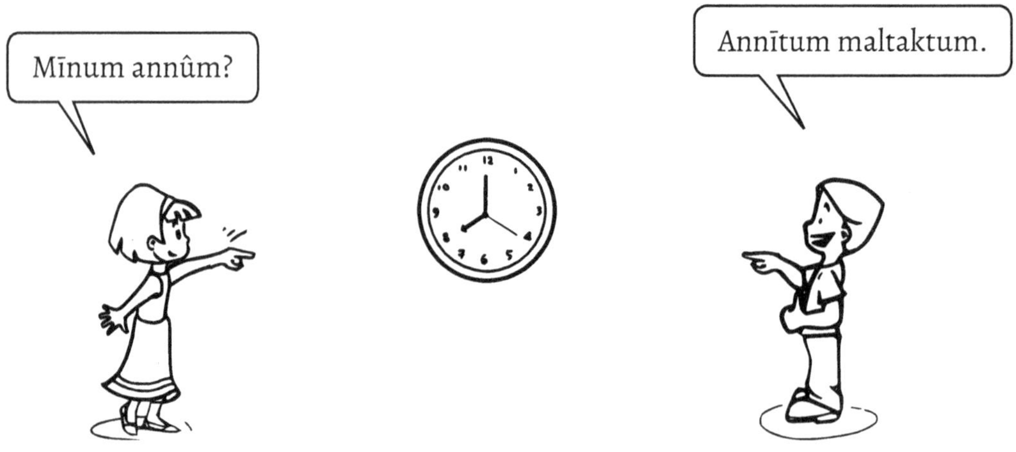

Mīnum annûm?

Annītum maltaktum.

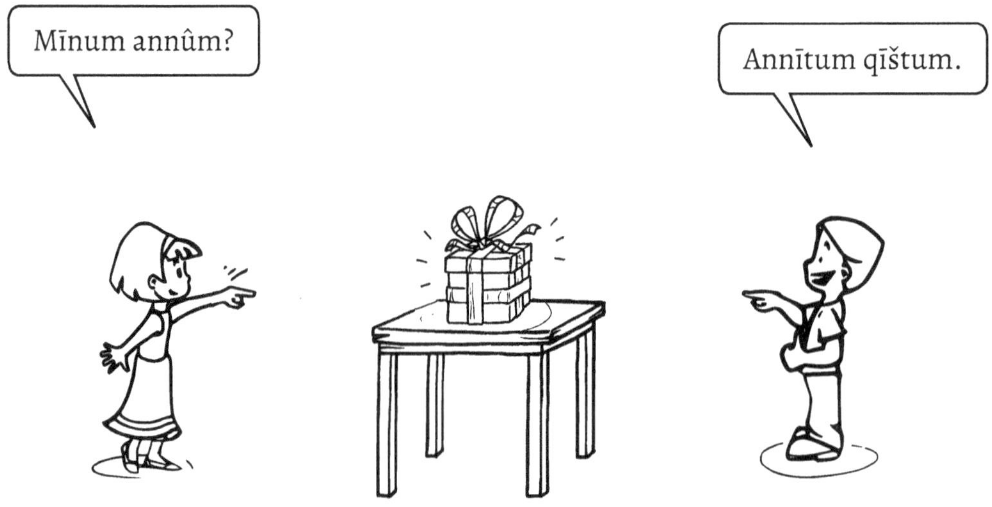

Mīnum annûm?

Annītum qīštum.

Ana aptim alkam!
Aptam pite!
Aptam edil!

1

2

Nērebum
Ana daltim alkam!
Nērebum
Daltam pite!

3

Nērebum
Ṣi!

Nērebum

B

1

2

3

C PETÛM, EDĒLUM, ERĒBUM, WAṢÛM

TO OPEN, TO CLOSE, TO ENTER, TO EXIT

1

2

3

4

5

6

C

TO OPEN, TO CLOSE,
TO ENTER, TO EXIT

1

2

3

4

5

6

D PETÛM, EDĒLUM, ELÛM, WARĀDUM

TO OPEN, TO CLOSE, TO WALK UP AND DOWN

D TO OPEN, TO CLOSE, TO WALK UP AND DOWN

Ṭuppam kullimīni!
1
Ṭuppam lupte!
2
Ṭuppam liqî!
3
Ṭuppam eli paššūrim šuknī!
4
Qanṭuppam kullimīni!
1
Qanṭuppam lupte!
2
Qanṭuppam liqi!
3
Qanṭuppam eli
paššūrim šukni!
4

1
2
3
4
1
2
3
4

Kāsam kullimīni!
1
Kāsam lupti!
2
Kāsam liqi!
3
Kāsam eli paššūrim šukni!
4
Karānam kullimīni!
1
Karānam luptī!
2
Karānam liqî!
3
Karānam eli paššūrim šukni!
4

Kussiam kullimanni!

Aptam kullimanni!

Paššūram kullimanni!

Talmīdam kullimīni!

E=MC²

Talmīttam kullimīni!

E=MC²

Mulammidam kullimīni!

E=MC²

$E=MC^2$
$E=MC^2$
$E=MC^2$

Ṭuppam kullimīni!

Qanṭuppam kullimīni!

Iṣurtam kullimīni!

Kāsam u laḫannam kullimīni!
H_2O

Ṭuppam rabīam u ṭuppam ṣeḫram kullimīni!

Qanṭuppam rabīam u qanṭuppam ṣeḫram kullimīni!

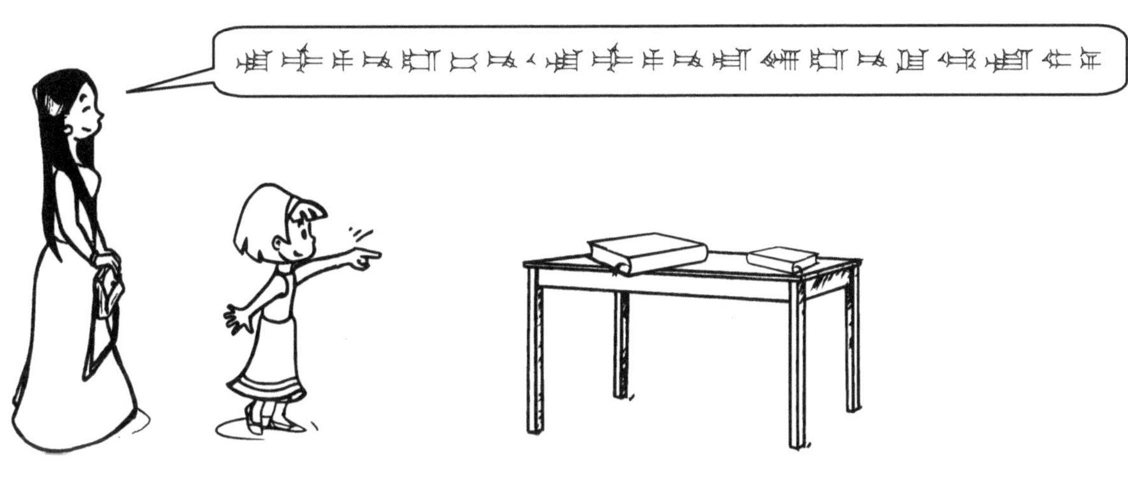

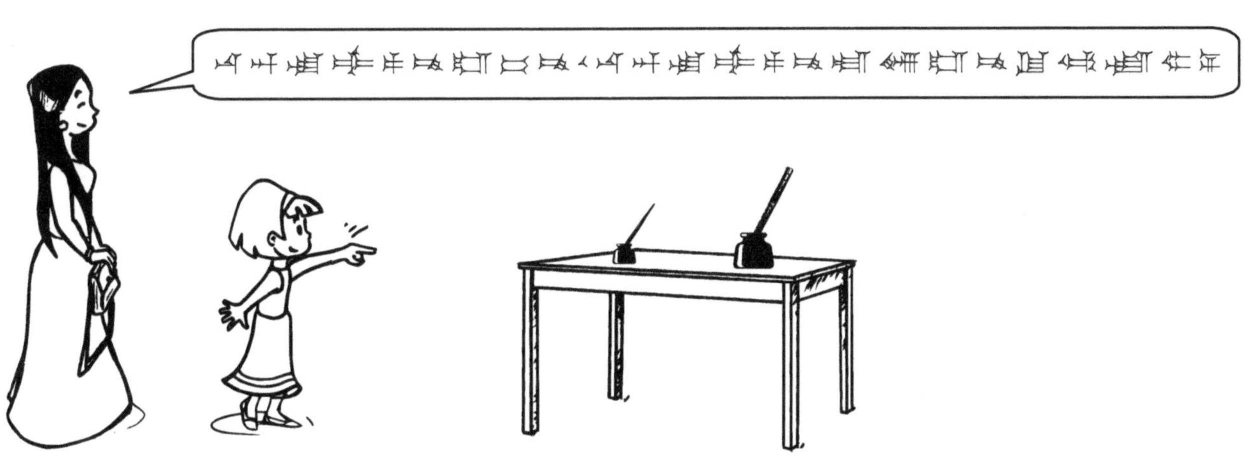

Awīlam u sinništam kullimīni!

Talmīdam mūdâm u
(talmīdam) lillam kullimīni!
E=MC²

Ḫarrānam maruštam u
ḫarrānam ṭābtam kullimīni!

$E=MC^2$
II=I+I

GRAMMATICA
GRAMMAR

1. Ištēn

Ištēn qanṭuppum

Ištēt naruqqum

Ištēt qištum

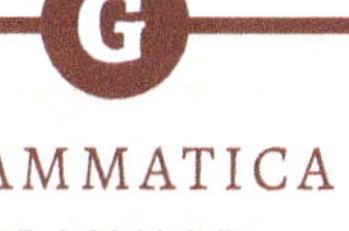

GRAMMATICA

GRAMMAR

2.

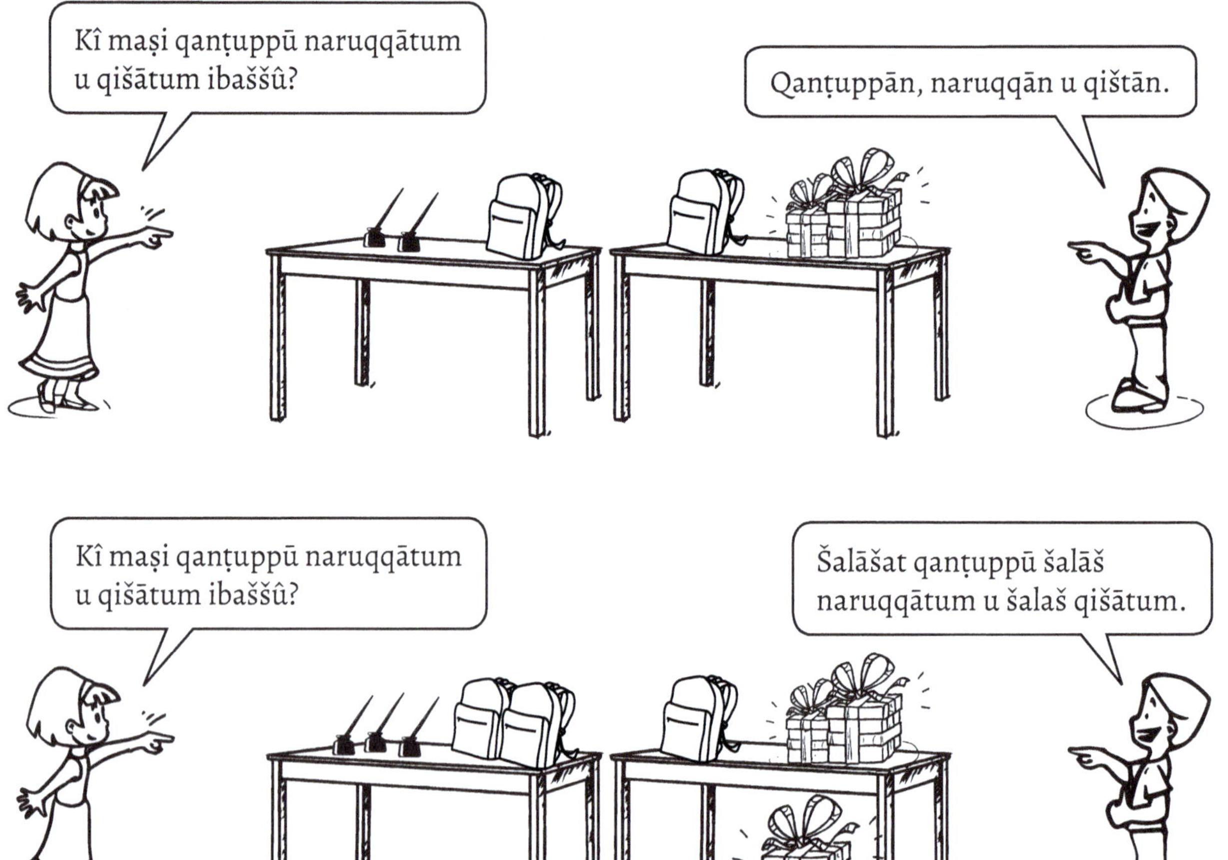

G

GRAMMATICA GRAMMAR

2. **Šinā**

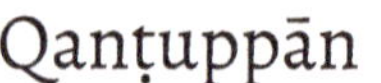

Qanṭuppān

Naruqqān

Qištān

3. **Šalaš**

Šalaš qanṭuppū

Šalaš naruqqātum

Šalaš qišātum

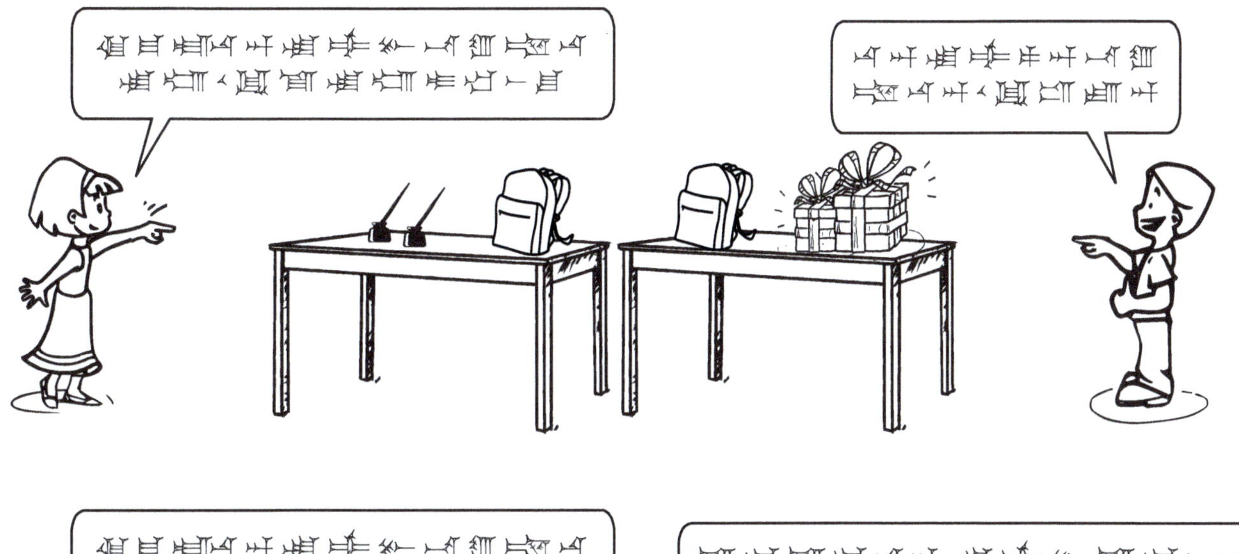

G

GRAMMATICA

GRAMMAR

2. 

3.

Kî maṣi qanṭuppū naruqqātum u qišātum ibaššû?

Erbet qanṭuppū u erbe naruqqātum u erbe qišātum.

Kî maṣi qanṭuppū naruqqātum u qišātum ibaššû?

Ḫamšat qanṭuppū ḫamiš naruqqātum u ḫamiš qišātum.

G

GRAMMATICA — GRAMMAR

4. **Erbe** — 5. **Ḫamiš**

Erbet qanṭuppū | Erbe naruqqātum | Erbe qišātum | Ḫamšat qanṭuppū | Ḫamiš naruqqātum | Ḫamiš qišātum

GRAMMATICA

GRAMMAR

4.

5. 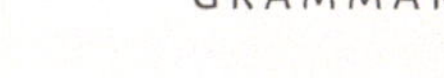

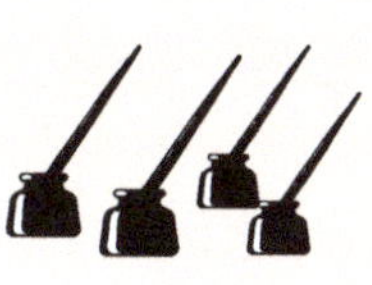

Ubānīkunu turṣā! Ubānīkunu kuppa!

Aḫīka turuṣ! Aḫīka kupup!

Rēška ulli! Rēška šuppil!

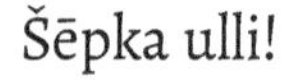
Šēpka ulli!
Qāt šumēlika ulli!
Būdka ulli!

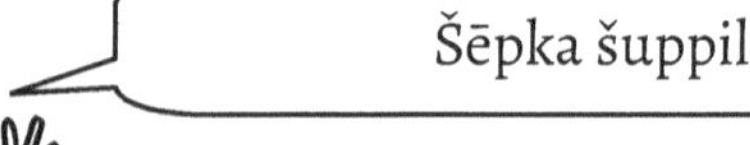
Šēpka šuppil!
Qāt imittika ulli!
Būdka šuppil!

Qātka luput!
Appaka luput!
Šinnīka luput!
Rēška luput!

Rēšum, rēšim, rēšam
Īnum, īnim, īnam
Uznum, uznim, uznam
Pûm, pîm, pīam
Būdum, būdim, būdam
Irtum, irtim, irtam
Purīdum, purīdim, purīdam
Birkum, birkim, birkam
Šārtum, šārtim, šārtam
Appum, appim, appam
Ubānum, ubānim, ubānam
Qātum, qātim, qātam
Aḫum, aḫim, aḫam
Kiṣir ammatim, kiṣir ammatim
šēpum, šēpim, šēpam

Pâka pite!
Dubub!
Rugum!
BLA BLA
BLA BLA...

Inglītam dubbā!
Paransitam dubbā!
Yaunītam dubbā!
Cheerio, my chap!
Vive la France!
Πῶς ἔχεις;

Zumur!
Hulul!
Nubuḫ!
BAU! BAU!

BLA BLA
BLA BLA...

Cheerio,
my chap!
Vive la
France!
Πῶς ἔχεις;

BAU!
BAU!

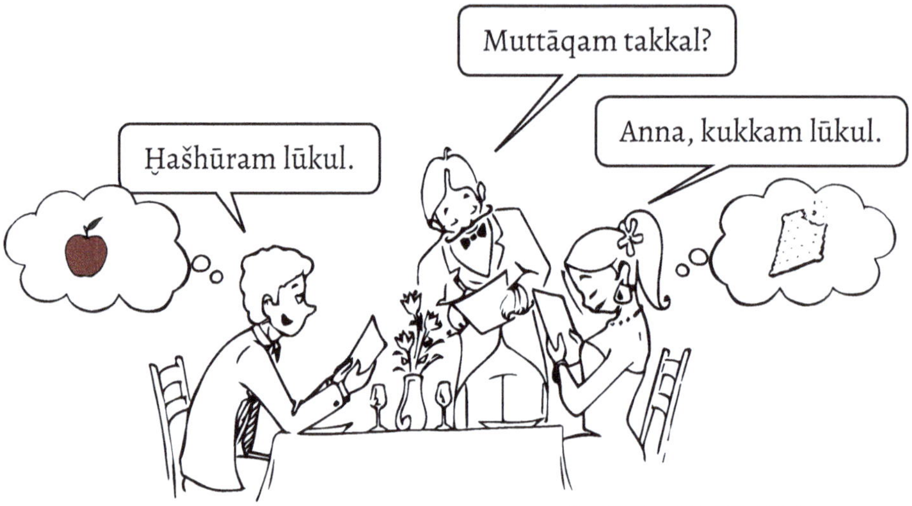

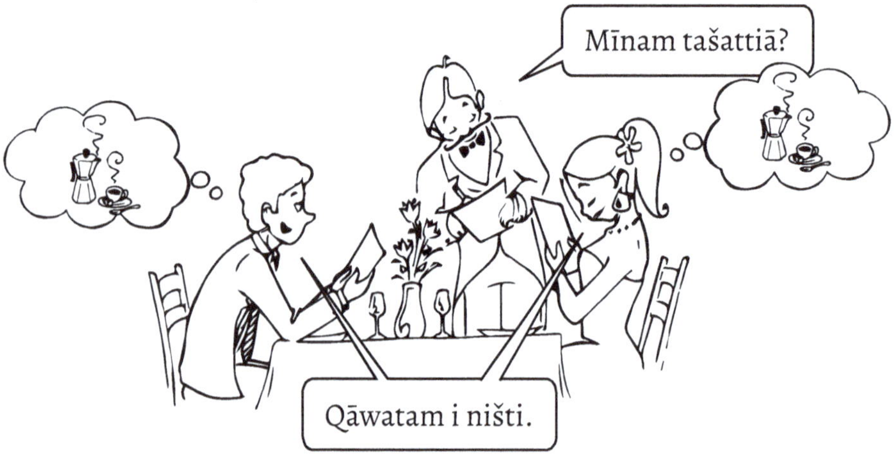

Muttāqam takkal?

Anna, kukkam lūkul.

Ḫašhūram lūkul.

Mīnam tašattiā?

Qāwatam i ništi.

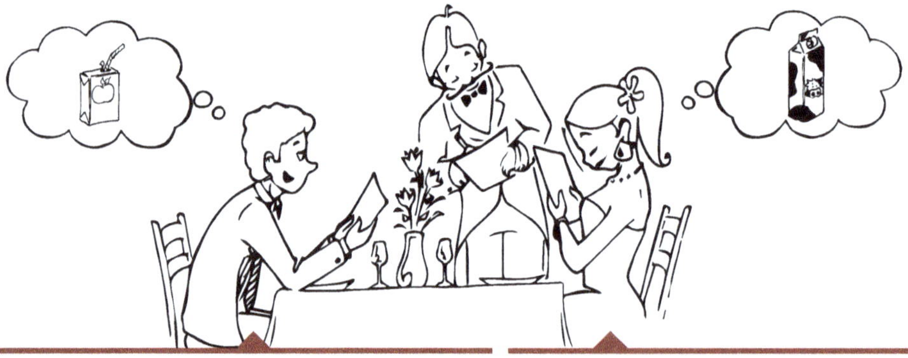

Bēlum, mīnam išatti? Mê ḫašḫūrim lišti.

Bēltum, mīnam išatti? Šizbam lišti.

Karānam išattû.

Mīnam takkal, takkalī?

Mīnam tašatti, tašattî?

Muttāqam takkal? Lūkul...

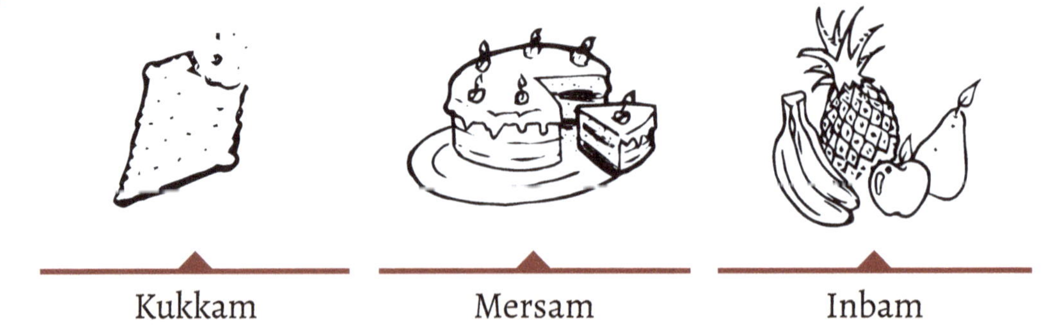

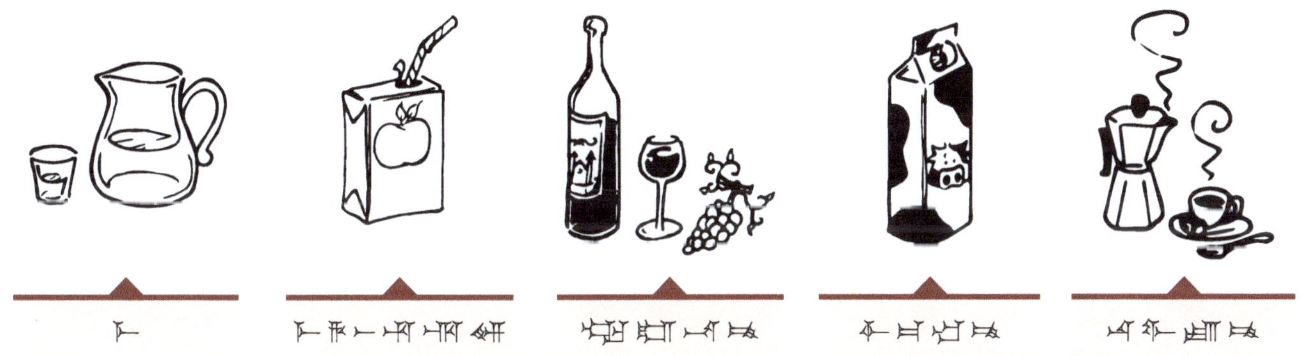

Mīnam ay īkul?
Ay ākul.
Nūnam takkal?
Nūnam ay īkul.
Mīnam līkul?
Nūnam takkalī?
Lūkul.
Nūnam līkul.
Lunūḫ.
Tupšarrūtam ay almad.

Bītam errub >< Bītam uṣṣi

Šamaš-mudammiq, Iapanītam dabābam tele''i?
Ballilītu, Iapanītam dabābam tele''î?
Ele''i.
Ul ele''i.
Šamaš-mudammiq, dabābam tele''i? Dubbā!
おはようございます
Bēl-abu-uṣur, lasāmam tele''i?
Gungunum, lasāmam tele''i?
Ele''i.
Ul ele''i.
Tele''i, Bēl-abu-uṣur? Lusum!
Ballilītu, šēpki našâm tele''î?
Ul ele''i.
Bēl-abu-uṣur, šēpka našâm tele''i?
Ele''i.
Šēpka iši!

おはようございます

Mīnam teppeš?
Lūkul. Bariāku.
Akul!
Akkal.
Mīnam teppeš?
Lūšti. Ṣamiāku.
Šiti!
Ašatti.
Kal ūmim dullam eppeš.
Kal ūmim ul akkal.
Bariāku.
Akkal.

Šamšum inappaḫ. Anumma ēm.

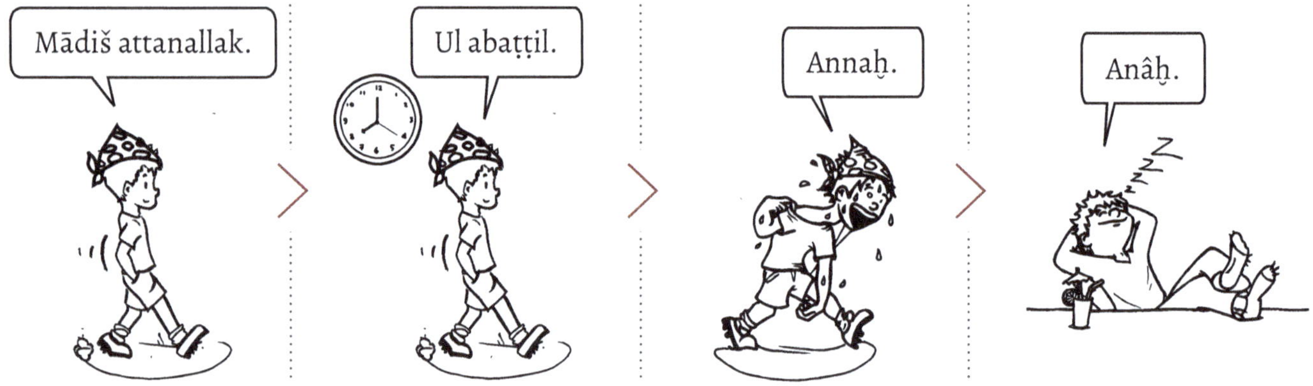

Mādiš attanallak.

Ul abaṭṭil.

Annaḫ.

Anâḫ.

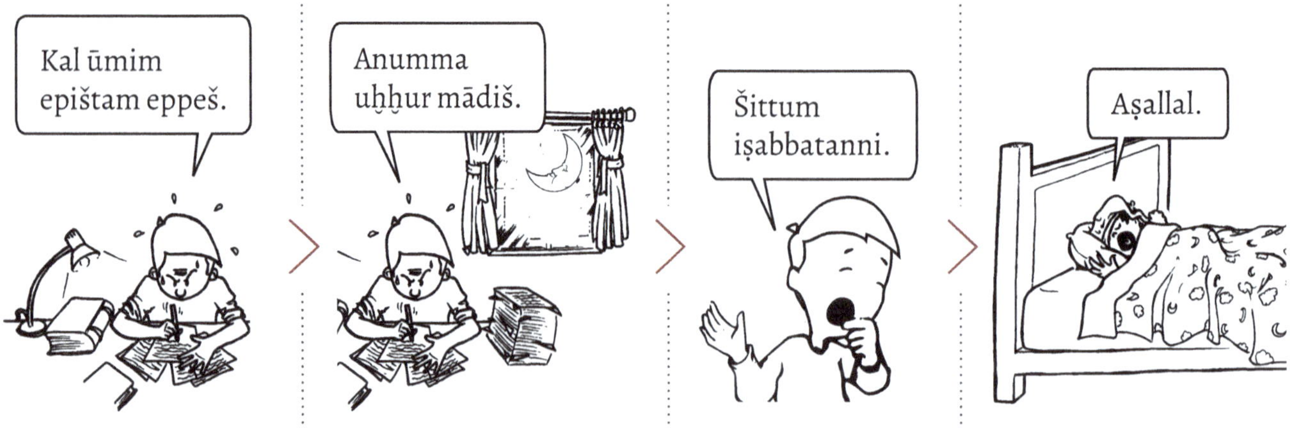

Kal ūmim epištam eppeš.

Anumma uḫḫur mādiš.

22.00 Anumma uḫḫur
24.00 Anumma uḫḫur mādiš.

Šittum iṣabbatanni.

Aṣallal.

22.00
24.00

MĪNUM ANNĪTUM?	*MĪNUM ANNÛM?*
annītum	**annûm**
aptum	kussûm
talmittum	paššūrum
naruqqum	lē'um
sinništum	kummum
qātum	laḫannum
iṣurtum	qanṭuppum
ubānum	talmīdum
appum	mulammidum
būdum	ṭuppum
īnum	zikarum
kāsum	awīlum
ḫašḫaltum	šamšum
maltaktum	nūnum
qīštum	ḫašḫūrum
daltum	karānum
šēpum	rāgim nesûtim
	aḫum
	pûm
	rēšum

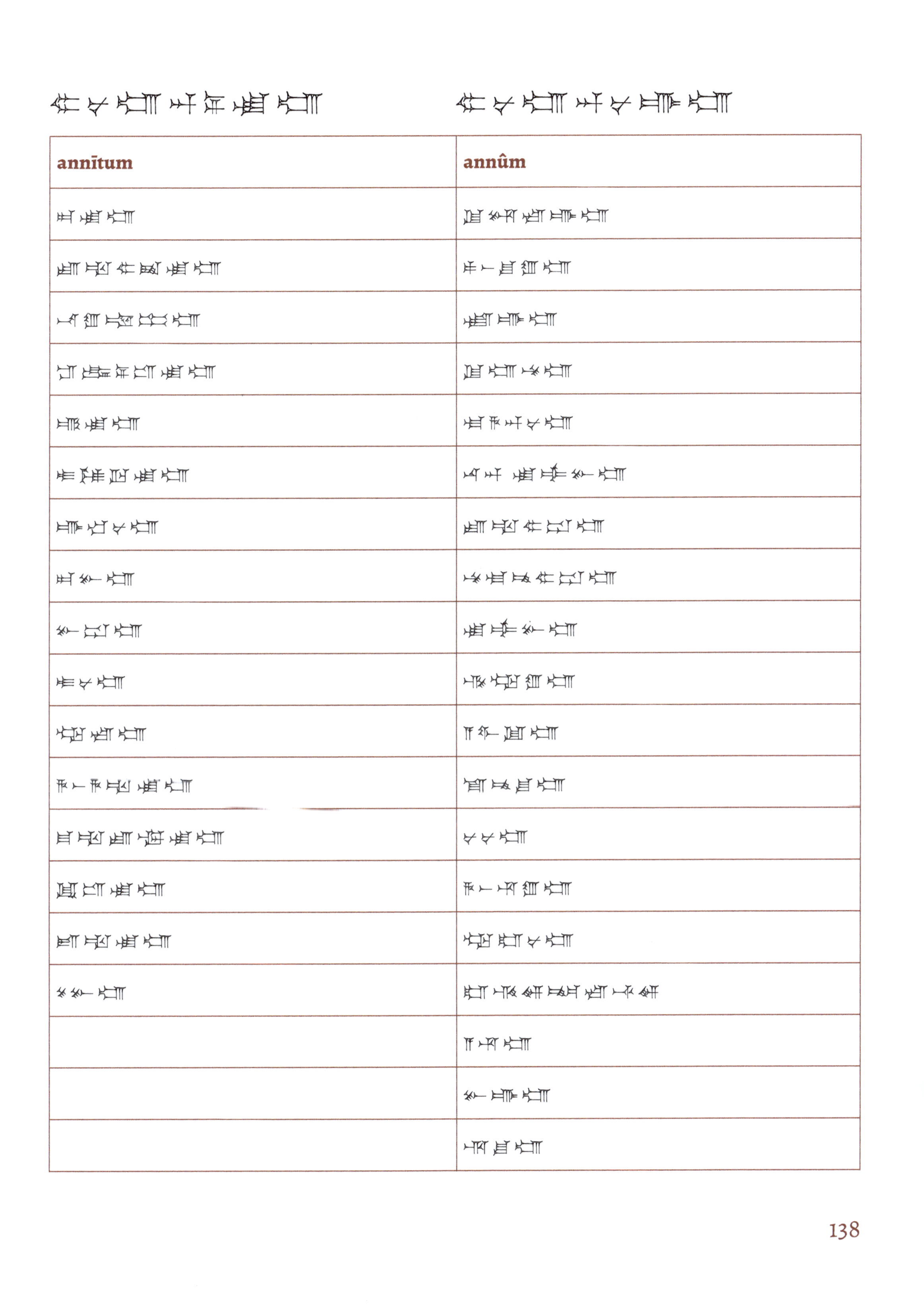

[illegible] [illegible]

annītum	annûm
[illegible]	[illegible]
[illegible]	[illegible]
[illegible]	[illegible]
[illegible]	[illegible]
[illegible]	[illegible]
[illegible]	[illegible]
[illegible]	[illegible]
[illegible]	[illegible]
[illegible]	[illegible]
[illegible]	[illegible]
[illegible]	[illegible]
[illegible]	[illegible]
[illegible]	[illegible]
[illegible]	[illegible]
[illegible]	[illegible]
[illegible]	[illegible]
	[illegible]
	[illegible]
	[illegible]

MĪNUM ANNĪTUM?

MĪNUM ANNÛM?

Annītum	**Annûm**
Aptam annītam	Kussiam anniam
Talmittam annītam	Paššūram anniam
Naruqqum annītam	Lēʾam anniam
Sinništum annītam	Kummam anniam
Qātam annītam	Laḫannam anniam
Iṣurtam annītam	Qanṭuppam anniam
Ubānam annītam	Talmīdam anniam
Appam annītam	Mulammidam anniam
Būdam annītam	Ṭuppam anniam
Īnam annītam	Zikaram anniam
Kāsam annītam	Awīlam anniam
Ḫašḫaltam annītam	Šamšam anniam
Maltaktam annītam	Nūnam anniam
Qīštam annītam	Ḫašḫūram anniam
Daltam annītam	Karānam anniam
Šēpam annītam	Rāgim nesûtim anniam
	Aḫam anniam
	Piam anniam
	Rēšam anniam

KÎ MAṢI NARUQQĀTUM IBAŠŠIĀ

Ištēt naruqqum	Naruqqān	Šalāš naruqqātum	Erbe naruqqātum	Ḫamiš naruqqātum

[illegible] [illegible]

Annītum	Annûm
[illegible]	[illegible]
[illegible]	[illegible]
[illegible]	[illegible]
[illegible]	[illegible]
[illegible]	[illegible]
[illegible]	[illegible]
[illegible]	[illegible]
[illegible]	[illegible]
[illegible]	[illegible]
[illegible]	[illegible]
[illegible]	[illegible]
[illegible]	[illegible]
[illegible]	[illegible]
[illegible]	[illegible]
[illegible]	[illegible]
[illegible]	[illegible]
	[illegible]
	[illegible]
	[illegible]

[illegible]

[illegible]	[illegible]	[illegible]
[illegible]	[illegible]	

KĪ MAṢI QANṬUPPŪ IBAŠŠŪ?

Ištēn qanṭuppum	Qanṭuppān	Šalāšat qanṭuppū	Erbet qanṭuppū	Ḫamšat qanṭuppū

ŠUM EPIŠTIM

Atallukum	Pasāsum	Šasûm
Leqûm	Alākum (+ ventive)	Alākum
Târum	Maḫāṣum	Lamādum
Edēlum	Petûm	Waṣûm
Dabābum	Kullumum	Elûm
Warādum	Barûm	Ragāmum
Lapātum	Šakānum	Ṣamûm
Ḫalālum	Baṭālum	Nâḫum
Ṣalālum	Nabāḫum	Zamārum
Ullûm	Epēšum	Akālum
Šatûm	Erēbum	Warûm
Qabûm		
Lušti	Ayyašti	Lišānam iapanītam dabābam ele''i
Muttāqam šiti	Nūnam akālam ē tašti	Sēpam ulliam tele''i
Mê ḫašḫūrim lišti	Mê ḫašḫūrim ayyišti	Lasāmam ile"i
Qāwatam i nīšti	Qāwatam e nīšti	Atallukam nile"i
Šizbam taštiā	Šizbam ē taštiā	Ḫalālam tele"iā
Karānam lištû	Karānam ayyištû	Ragāmam ile"û

AŠŠUM BĪTIM

Ana bītim erub	Ištu bītim ṣi	Ina bītim anāku

[illegible]

[illegible]	[illegible]	[illegible]
[illegible]	[illegible]	

[illegible]

[illegible]	[illegible]	[illegible]
[illegible]	[illegible]	[illegible]
[illegible]	[illegible]	[illegible]
[illegible]	[illegible]	[illegible]
[illegible]	[illegible]	[illegible]
[illegible]	[illegible]	[illegible]
[illegible]	[illegible]	[illegible]
[illegible]	[illegible]	[illegible]
[illegible]	[illegible]	[illegible]
[illegible]	[illegible]	[illegible]
[illegible]	[illegible]	[illegible]
[illegible]		
[illegible]	[illegible]	[illegible]
[illegible]	[illegible]	[illegible]
[illegible]	[illegible]	[illegible]
[illegible]	[illegible]	[illegible]
[illegible]	[illegible]	[illegible]
[illegible]	[illegible]	[illegible]

[illegible]

[illegible]	[illegible]	[illegible]

3 Adnātam esēqum

DESCRIBING THE WORLD

A IBAŠŠI U UL IBAŠŠI

PRESENCE AND ABSENCE

3

DESCRIBING THE WORLD

A PRESENCE AND ABSENCE

Ullûm qanṭuppum?
Ullûm ul qanṭuppum.
ULLÛM

Annûm ṭuppûm?
Annûm ul ṭuppum.
ANNÛM

Bēl-abu-uṣur wašbāta?
Hašda'ītu wašbāti?
Wašbāku, mulammidum.
Bēl-abu-uṣur
Hašda'ītu
Ballilītu
Ballilītu wašbāt?
Ballilītu lā wašbat.

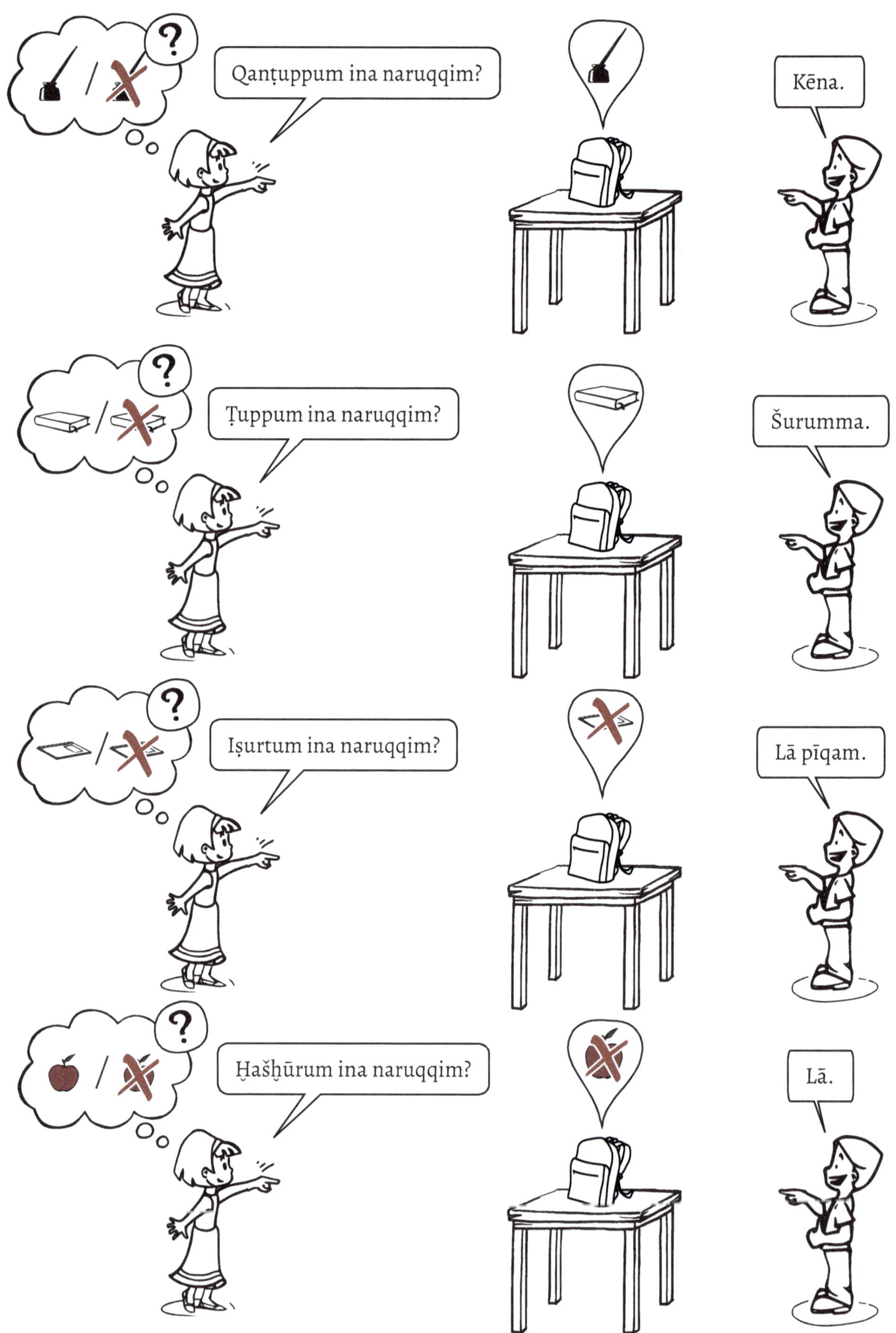
Qanṭuppum ina naruqqim?
Kēna.
Ṭuppum ina naruqqim?
Šurumma.
Iṣurtum ina naruqqim?
Lā pīqam.
Ḫašḫūrum ina naruqqim?
Lā.

Qanṭuppum ina naruqqim?
Anna.
Iṣurtum ina naruqqim?
Šurumma.
Annûm mulammidum?
Anna.
Mulammidatum atti?
Lā.
Lā
Lā pīqam
Kēna
Anna
Šurumma

Ullûm qanṭuppum?
Annûtum qanṭuppū.

Qanṭuppam
šuāti idnīm!

Ullûm ṭuppum?
Annûtu ṭuppū.

Ṭuppam šuāti idnīm!

Paššūrum šū ayyikīam?
Paššūram anaṭṭal.

Annûma.

Šurānum šū ayyikīam?
Šurānam anaṭṭal.

Annûma.

6. **Šeššet (m) / Šediš (f)**

Šeššet qanṭuppū

7. **Sebet (m) / Sebe (f)**

Sebe naruqqātum

8. **Samānat (m) / Samāne (f)**

Samāne qišātum

9. **Tišīt (m) / Tiše (f)**

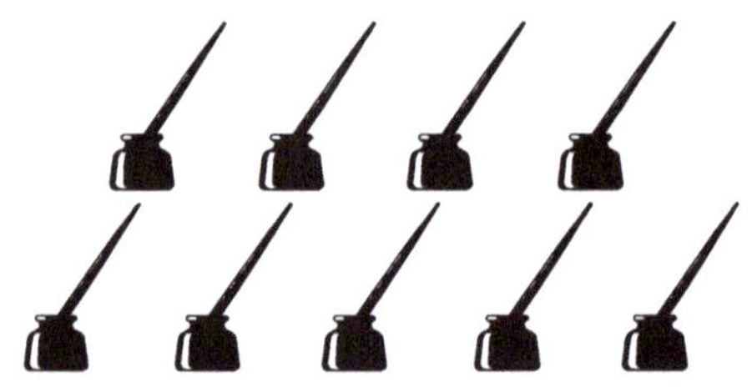

Tišīt qanṭuppū

10. **Ešret (m) / Ešer (f)**

Masculine		**Feminine**	
1	ištēn	**1**	ištēt
2	šinā	**2**	šittā
3	šalāš	**3**	šalāšt
4	erbe	**4**	erbet
5	ḫamiš	**5**	ḫamšat
6	šediš	**6**	šeššet
7	sebe	**7**	sebet
8	samāne	**8**	samānat
9	tiše	**9**	tišīt
10	ešer	**10**	ešret

6. [illegible] / [illegible]

[illegible]

7. [illegible] / [illegible]

[illegible]

8. [illegible] / [illegible]

[illegible]

9. [illegible] / [illegible]

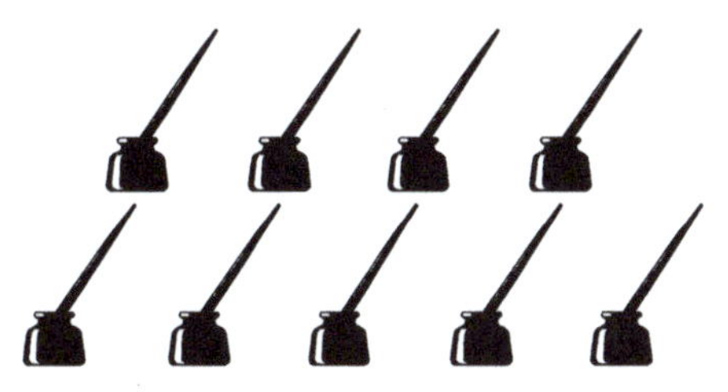

[illegible]

10. [illegible] / [illegible]

Masculine		Feminine	
1	[illegible]	1	[illegible]
2	[illegible]	2	[illegible]
3	[illegible]	3	[illegible]
4	[illegible]	4	[illegible]
5	[illegible]	5	[illegible]
6	[illegible]	6	[illegible]
7	[illegible]	7	[illegible]
8	[illegible]	8	[illegible]
9	[illegible]	9	[illegible]
10	[illegible]	10	[illegible]

Kī maṣi qanṭuppū ibaššū?
Šina qanṭuppū ibaššū.

Kī maṣi paššūrū ibaššū?
Šalāšat paššūrū ibaššū.

Kī maṣi qīšātum ibaššiā?
Šalāš qīšātum ibaššiā.

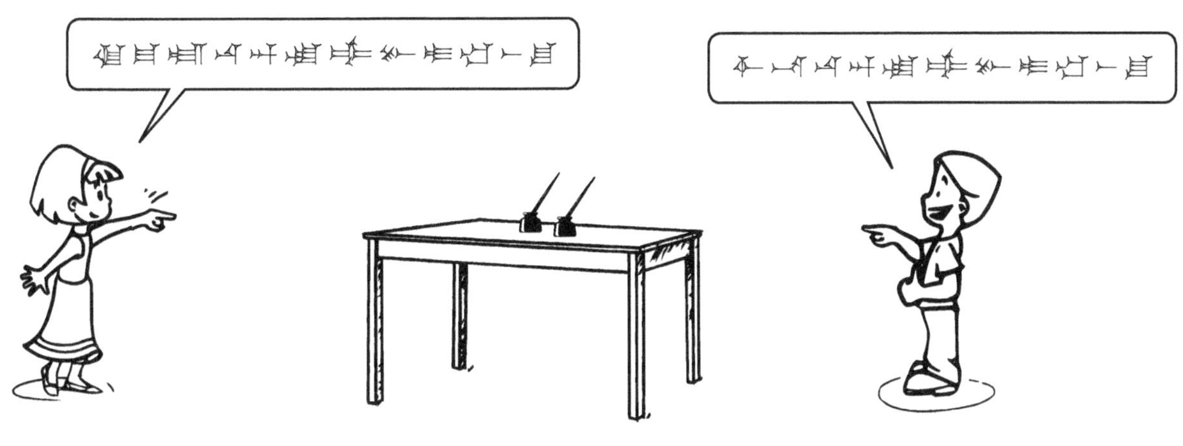

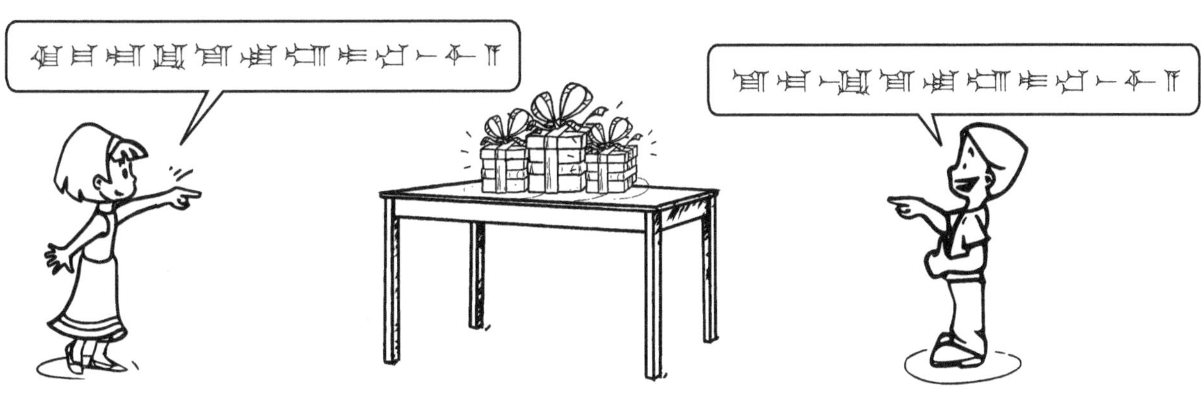

* = Kī maṣi qanṭuppū ina qātiki? Šalāšat qanṭuppū ina qātiya.

** = Kī maṣi ṭuppū ina qātiki? Erbet ṭuppū ina qātiya.

Pērtī arkat.

Pērtī kurīat.

Pērtī išrat.

Pērtī qunnunat
u zaqnāku.

Gubbuḫāku.

D KUṢṢUM U UMŠUM, PULUḪTUM U MURṢUM

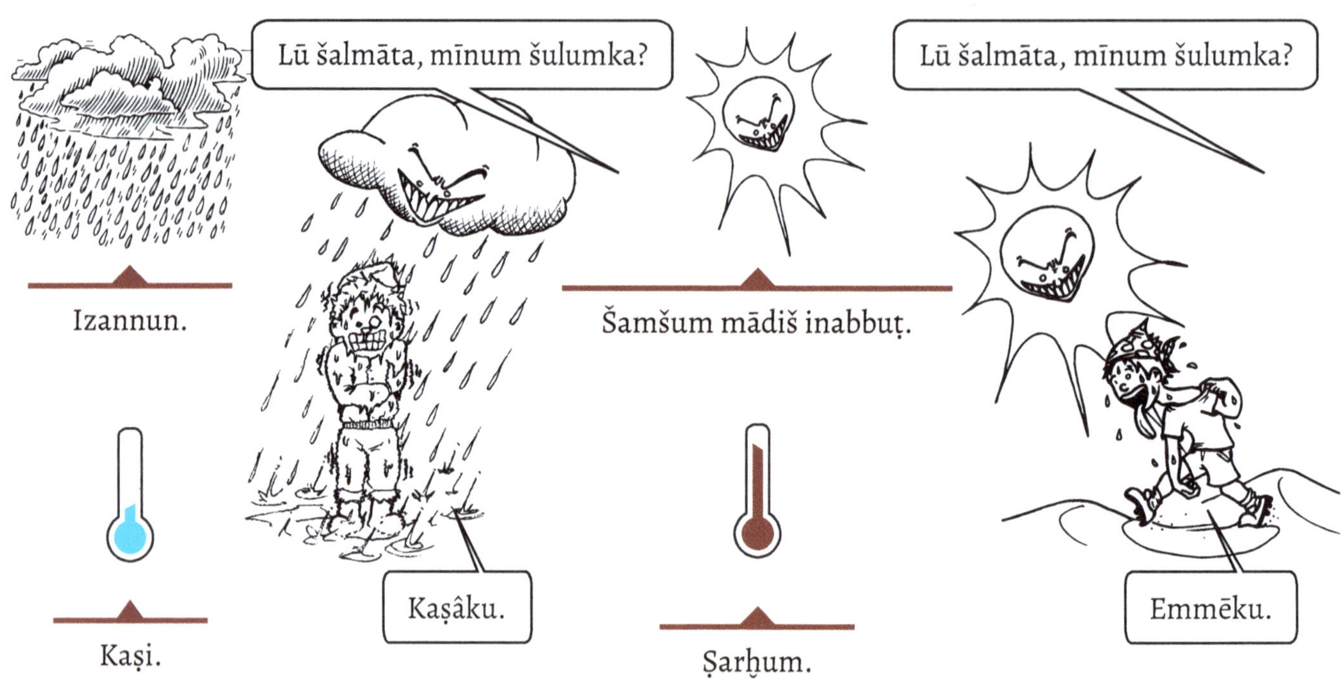

D COLD AND HEAT, FEAR AND PAIN.

1
Ayyišam tallak?
Ina sūqim allak.
2
Mīnam tammar?
Eṭemmu ammar.
3
Mīnum ibaššīkum?
Palḫāku.
4
Warki quppim apazzar.
Ayyikī'am tapazzar?
Mīnam takkal?
Imtam akkal.
Mīnam tašatti?
Mašqītam ašatti.
Lū šalmāta,
mīnum šulumka?
Abluṭ.
Mīnum ibaššīkum?
Rēšī maruṣ.
Mīnum ibaššīkum?
Libbī maruṣ.

1
2
3
4

Bēl-abu-uṣur itebbe.

Bēl-abu-uṣur illak.

Bēl-abu-uṣur ibaṭṭil.

Bēl-abu-uṣur uššab.

Bēl-abu-uṣur itebbe.

Bēl-abu-uṣur ilassum.

Bēl-abu-uṣur ina muḫḫi lē'im išaṭṭar.

Mīnam Bēl-abu-uṣur ippeš? Bēl-abu-uṣur itebbe.

Bēl-abu-uṣur illak.

Bēl-abu-uṣur išaḫḫiṭ.

Bēl-abu-uṣur uššab.

1
2
3
4
1
2
3
4

1

Bēl-abu-uṣur illak.

2

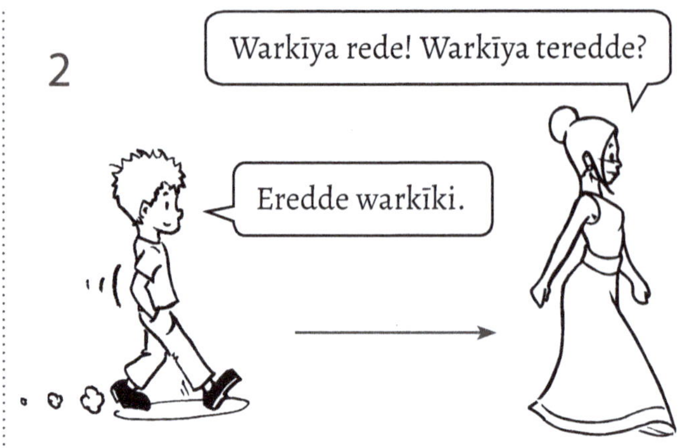

Bēl-abu-uṣur iredde.

3

Bēl-abu-uṣur issaḫḫur.

4

Bēl-abu-uṣur illak.

F MAŠ'ALĀTUM "IŠTU AYYĀNIM" U "ANA AYYĀNIM"

'WHERE FROM?' AND 'WHERE TO?'

F 'WHERE FROM?' AND 'WHERE TO?'

Bēl-abu-uṣur annīki'am illak.

Bēl-abu-uṣur ullīkiam illak.

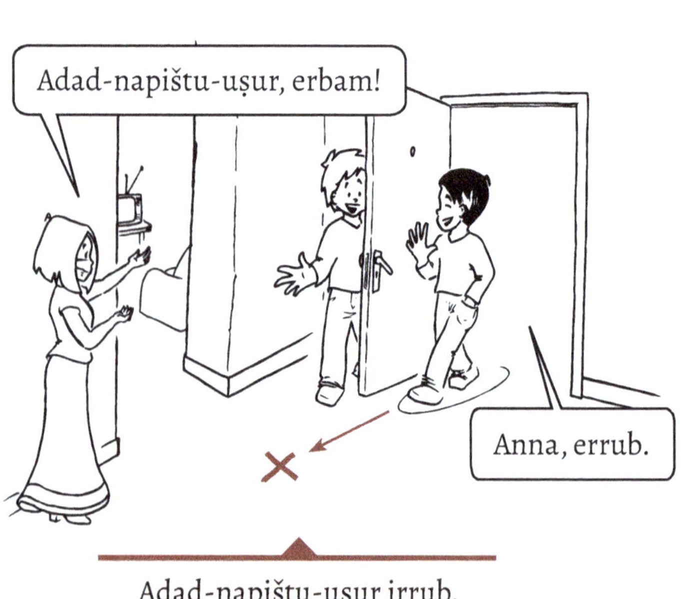

Adad-napištu-uṣur irrub.

Hašda'ītu ullīkiam uṣṣî.

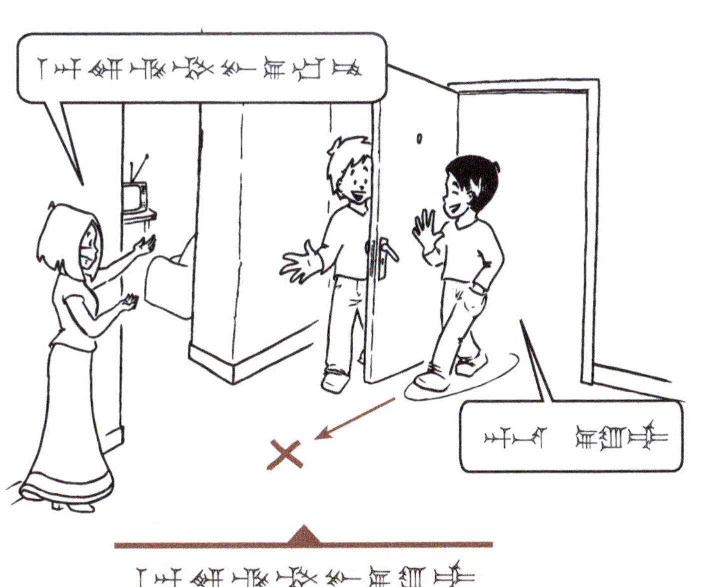

Bēl-abu-uṣur illakam.

Bēl-abu-uṣur ullīkiam illik.

Adad-napištu-uṣur ištu kirîm illak.

Adad-napištu-uṣur bītam irrub.
Ina bītim aḫum u ummum.

Bēl-abu-uṣur ina bītim uṣṣi.

Bēl-abu-uṣur ayyānum illak?
Bēl-abu-uṣur narqabtam irrub.

Ina + genitive = in / out off (from / in)	Ina kummim, ina bītim, ina narqabtim!
Accusative without preposition	Kummam, bītam, narqabtam erub!

Bēl-abu-uṣur ana kirîm illak.

Bēl-abu-uṣur kiriam irrub.

Bēl-abu-uṣur ina kirîm.

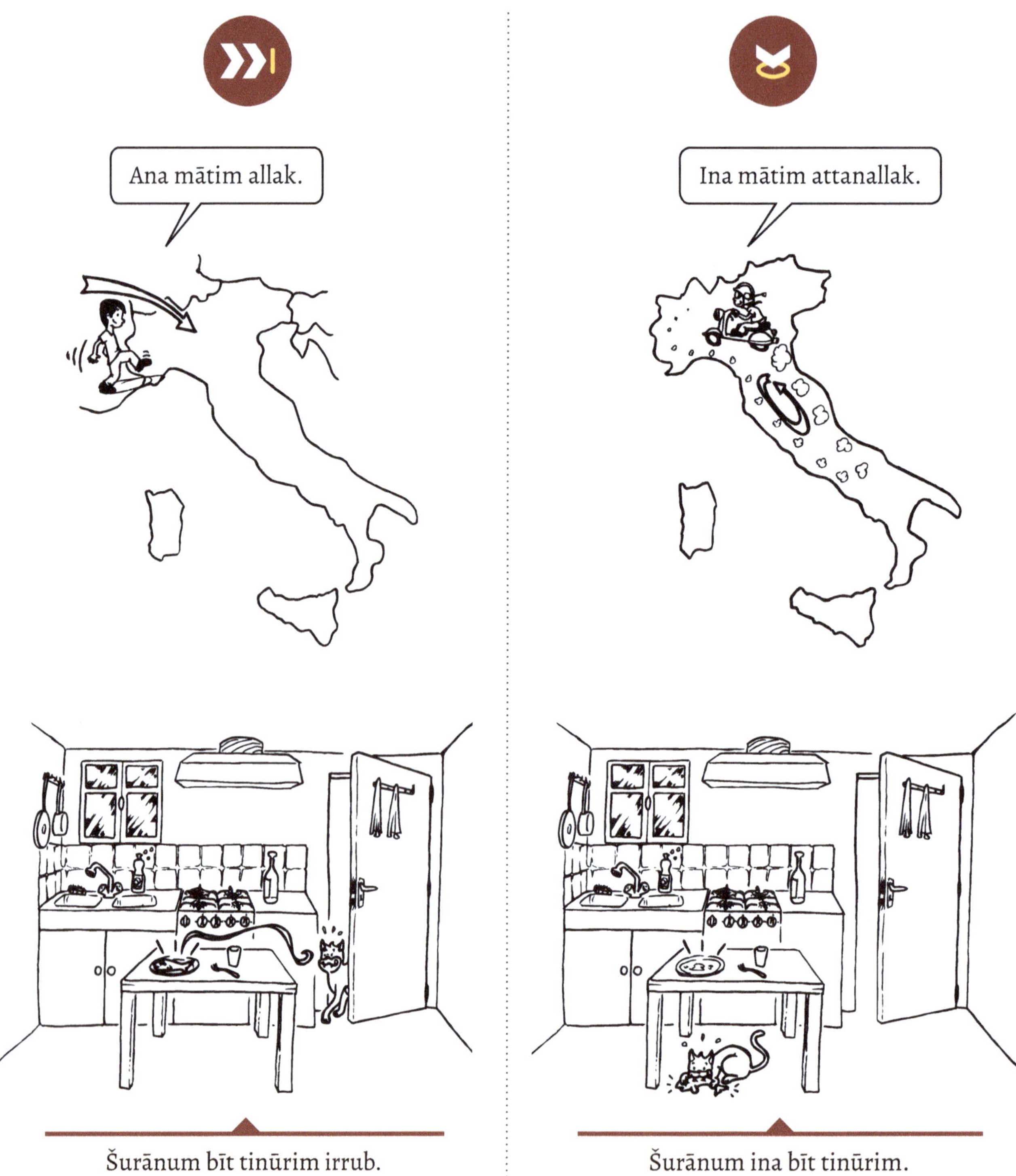

Šurānum bīt tinūrim irrub.

Šurānum ina bīt tinūrim.

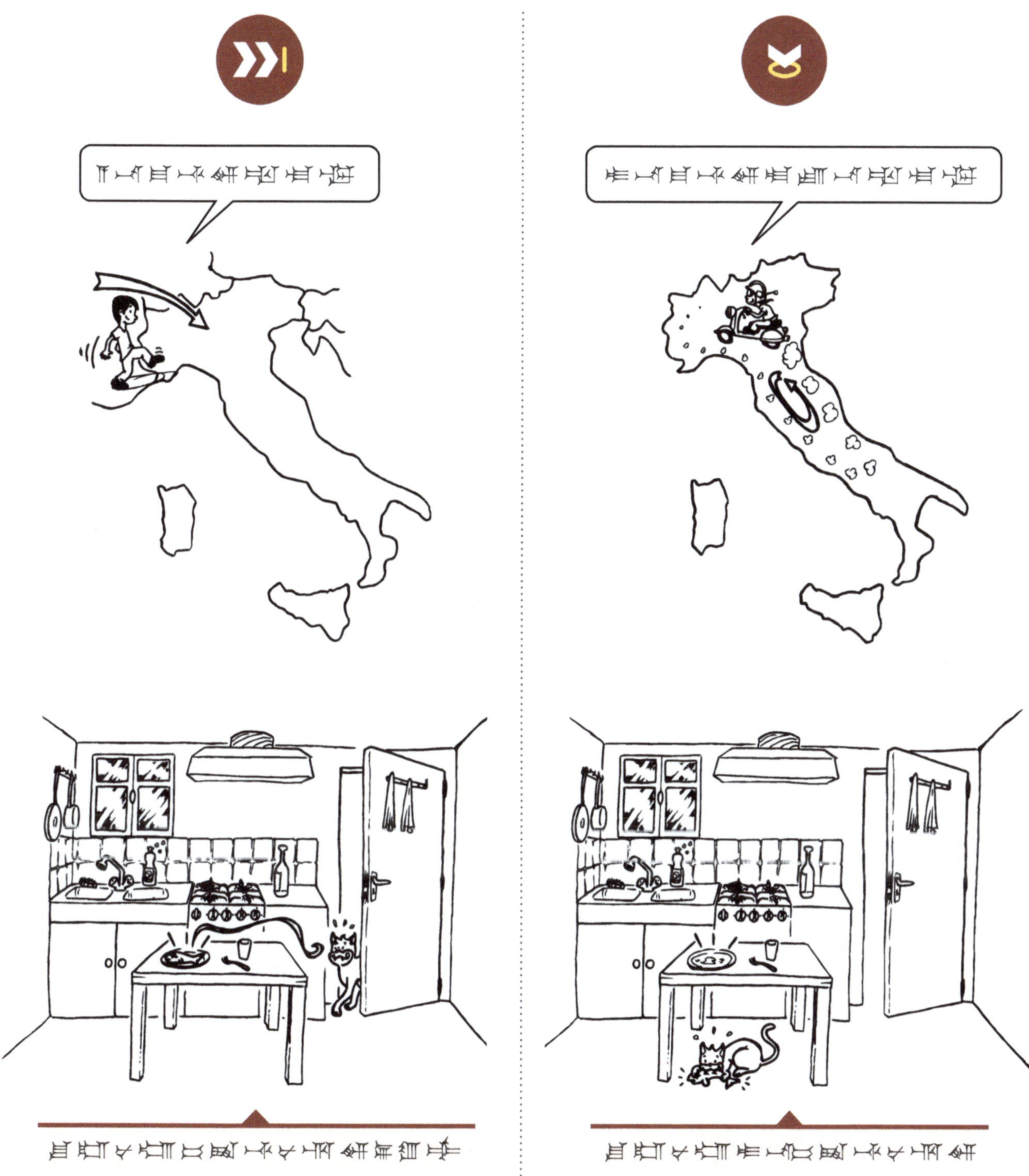

Bēl-abu-uṣur ina kirîm uṣṣi.

Bēl-abu-uṣur ištu kirîm illak.

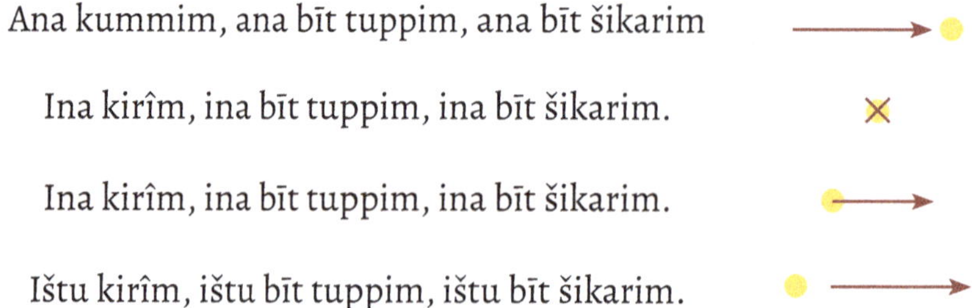

Ana kummim, ana bīt tuppim, ana bīt šikarim

Ina kirîm, ina bīt tuppim, ina bīt šikarim.

Ina kirîm, ina bīt tuppim, ina bīt šikarim.

Ištu kirîm, ištu bīt tuppim, ištu bīt šikarim.

Gudādītu ina bīt apê.

Gimil-Nergal ištu girginakkim illak.

Bēl-abu-uṣur ištu maḫīrim illak.

Gudādītu itti ummim ana bīt ṭuppim illak.

Bēl-abu-uṣur ina bīt kaspim irrub.

Bēl-abu-uṣur ištu bābtim illak

Ana bīt qerītim alik.

Watartīn ana girginakkim rikab.
Watartīn

Narkabtam ana bīt gabê rikab.
Narkabtum.

Illatum
Ina illatim ana bīt šikarim rikab.

Rukūbum.
Rukūbam ana maḫīrim rikab.
$ $ $

Bēl-abu-uṣur illi.

Bēl-abu-uṣur urrad.

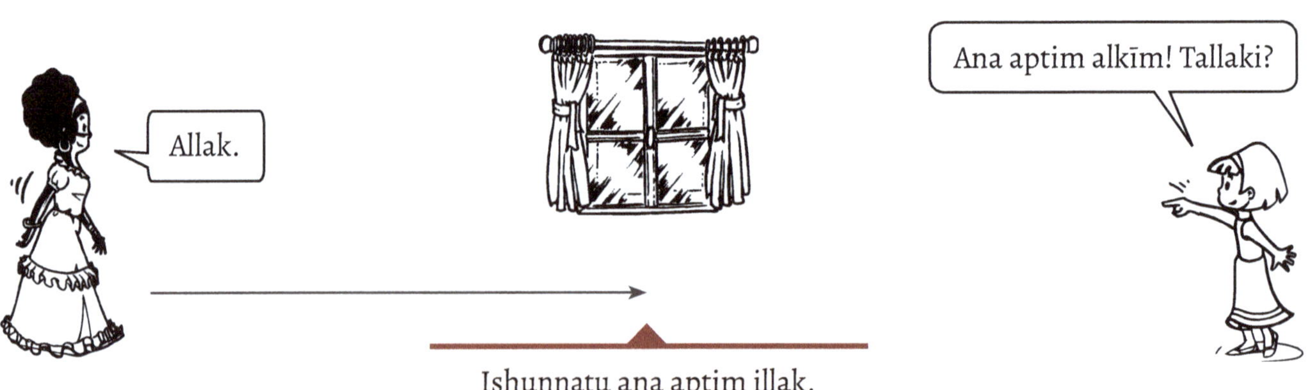

Ishunnatu ana aptim illak.

Ishunnatu aptam ipette.

Ishunnatu aptam iddil.

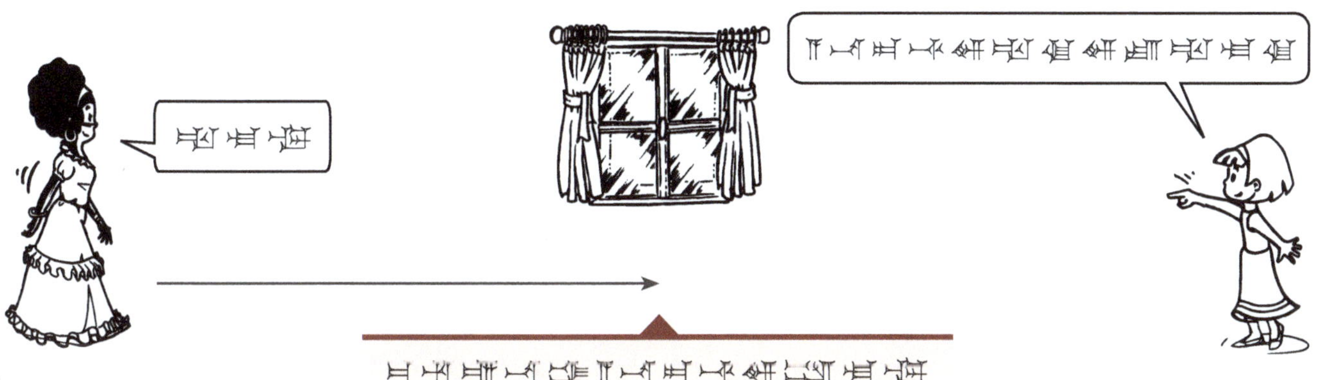

Bēl-abu-uṣur ana daltim illak .

Bēl-abu-uṣur daltam ipette.

Mārum uṣṣi. Mārtum daltam ukallam.

Bēl-abu-uṣur daltam imaḫḫaṣ.

Bēl-abu-uṣur daltam ipette.

Bēl-abu-uṣur kummam irrub.

Bēl-abu-uṣur daltam iddil.

Bēl-abu-uṣur daltam ipette.

Bēl-abu-uṣur ištu kummim uṣṣi.

NÊREBUM

Šamaš-mudammiq ḫašḫūram ileqqe.

Šamaš-mudammiq ḫašḫūram ikkal.

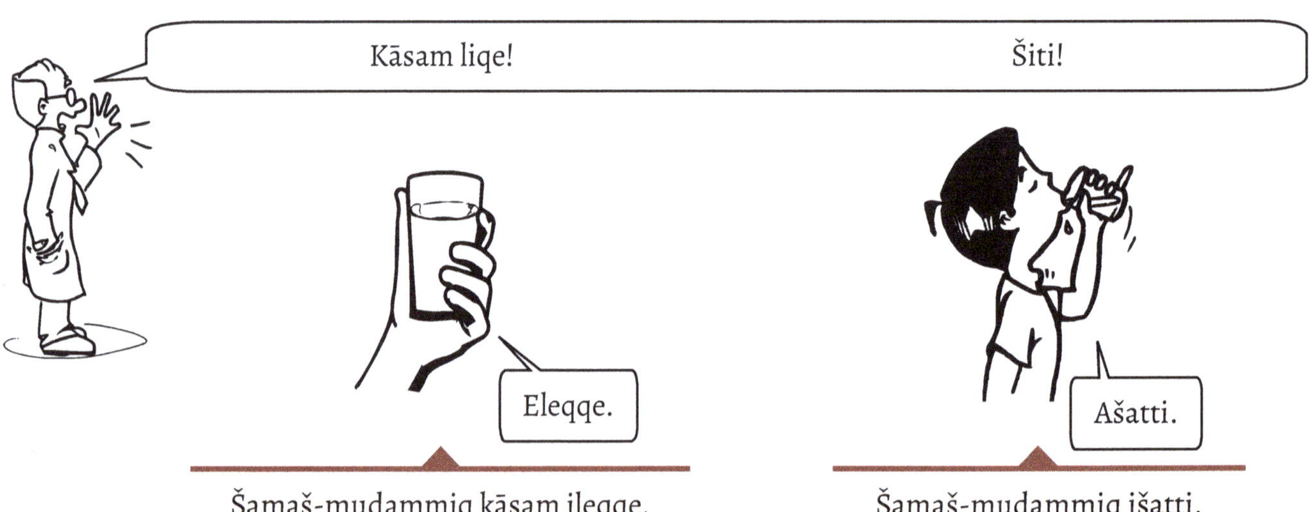

Šamaš-mudammiq kāsam ileqqe.

Šamaš-mudammiq išatti.

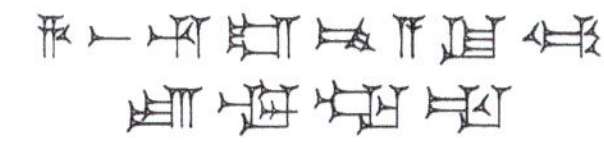

Bēl-abu-uṣur ṭuppašu iše''e.

Bēl-abu-uṣur ṭuppam immar.

Bēl-abu-uṣur ṭuppam ana mulammidim inaddin.

Bēl-abu-uṣur ṭuppašu imaḫḫar.

1

2

3

4

Atallukum	**Pasāsum**	**Še'ûm**	**Leqûm**	**Šemûm**	**Alākum**
Attanallak	Apassas	Eše''i	Eleqqe	Ešemme	Allak
Tattanallak	Tapassas	Teše''i	Teleqqe	Tešemme	Tallak
Ittanallak	Ipassas	Iše''i	Ileqqe	Išemme	Illak

BLA BLA
BLA BLA...

1

Bēl-abu-uṣur ul ilassum-ma ittanallak.

2

Bēl-abu-uṣur maltakassu inaṭṭal.

3

Bēl-abu-uṣur ul ittanallak-ma ilassum.

4

Bēl-abu-uṣur aniḫ.

1

Bēl-abu-uṣur dalat mulammidim imaḫḫaṣ.

2

Bēl-abu-uṣur daltam ipette.

3

Bēl-abu-uṣur ina rigim mulammidim ul idaggal uqqī-ma irrub.

4

Mulammidum innip.

1

[illegible]

2

[illegible]

3

[illegible]

4

[illegible]

1

[illegible]

2

[illegible]

3

[illegible]

4

[illegible]

1

Bānītu-rēṣûa ulla nalbašamma naḫlaptam labšat.

2

Bānītu-rēṣûa ulla ša ṣillimma naruqqam ušelli.

3

Bānītu-rēṣûa ištu bītim uṣṣi.

LIBBI AWÂTIM
VOCABULARY

Naruqqum

Ṣillum

Naḫlaptum

Nalbašum

1

VOCABULARY

2

3

1
Pānûm etebbe.

2
Warka allak.

3
Warka abaṭṭil.

4
Warka uššab.

Mīnam pānûm teppeš.
Pānûm etebbe.

Mīnam warka teppeš?
Warka allak.

Mīnam warka teppeš?
Warka abaṭṭal u uššab.

1
Pānûm daltam amaḫḫaṣ.

2
Warka ina rigim mulammidim uqqi umma “erbam”.
Erub!

3
Warka daltam epette.

4
Warka errub.

5
Pānûm daltam tepette?
Ulla. Pānûm daltam amaḫḫaṣ, warka rigim mulammidim uqqi, umma “erbam”, warka daltam epette.

H

Qātam ana zamārim iškun.
Zamāram uštarda.
Zamāram ipparraku.
Qātam ana šasîm iškun.
Šasâm uštarda.
Šasâm ipparraku.
Qātam ana šaḫāṭim iškun.
Šaḫāṭam uštarda.
Šaḫāṭam ipparraku.

Mīnum epištaka?

Asû.

Mulammittum.

Mukīl abbūti.

Nuḫatimmum.

Anāku Ninurta-ušebši,
ištu māt Tâmtim eliāku.
Bīt asûtim.
Asûm anāku. Šipram
ina bīt asûtim eppeš.

Anāku Rīḫtāya.
Ištu māt Amurrim eliāku.
Mulammittum anāku.
Šipram ina bīt ṭuppī eppeš.

Damqiš azammar.
Anḫāku.

Damqiš aḫallul.
Beriāku.

www.ingramcontent.com/pod-product-compliance
Lightning Source LLC
Chambersburg PA
CBHW061037241225
37277CB00034B/262
9789657698211